Educating
 for
Responsible Action

Educating
for
Responsible Action

by
NICHOLAS P. WOLTERSTORFF

CSI PUBLICATIONS
WM. B. EERDMANS PUBLISHING COMPANY

Copyright © 1980 by Christian Schools International
3350 East Paris Avenue SE, Grand Rapids, MI 49508
P. O. Box 39, Norwich, Ontario NOJ 1PO
All rights reserved
Printed in the United States of America

Published jointly by Christian Schools International and
Wm. B. Eerdmans Publishing Co., 255 Jefferson Avenue
SE, Grand Rapids MI 49503.

Library of Congress Cataloging in Publication Data

Wolterstorff, Nicholas.
  Educating for responsible action.

  Commissioned by Christian Schools International.
  1. Moral education.   2. Christian education—
Philosophy.   I. Christian Schools International.
II. Title.
LC268.W68   370.11′4   80-24035
ISBN 0-8028-1857-9 (Eerdmans)

Contents

Preface

From the beginning of the Christian church, Christian parents have considered it desirable and even obligatory to educate their children so as to induct them into the vision and life of the Christian community. In this they have acted in the same way as the members of any other religiously or ideologically unified community. True, some have dissented from this, holding that they should instead, with full impartiality, present to their children all the major life views confronting humanity. But most Christian parents have thought of their children not as outsiders to the community but as members of it already. They have accordingly sought to give them a Christian education.

This book presents a certain facet of Christian education. Commissioned by Christian Schools International, an association of Christian day schools in the Calvinist tradition, it is for the most part as relevant to church education and to the informal teaching and learning that takes place in the Christian family as it is to formal day school education. And throughout it is as relevant to other traditions of Christianity as to the Calvinist. Indeed, in the central part of the book, we offer a perspective applicable to education generally, not just to Christian education. Admittedly, not all will agree with the perspective articulated there, for it is a perspective intentionally framed to comport with the Christian vision. But in failing to gain universal consent it merely shares the general fate of perspectives on education.

The facet or dimension of Christian education presented in this book is that of tendency learning—that is, learning in which the student acquires tendencies to action. This is called *decisional learning* in some of the publications of Christian Schools International, where it is described as learning which consists of growth in right choosing, in accepting or rejecting what *is* in the light of what things *ought to be*. It includes moral and aesthetic, legal and logical choosing, based on relevant Christian standards. Included in this dimension is growth in appreciation, attitude, judgment, and commitment.*

The focus of this book is thus limited. It discusses just one phase of pedagogy, namely, the pedagogy for tendency (or "decisional") teaching and learning. It is not concerned with pedagogy in general, only with the pedagogy for inculcating tendencies or dispositions to action. And except for illustrative examples, the primary concern is not with curriculum. The aim is to discover effective and responsible strategies for inculcating tendencies to action. There is no attempt here to say *what* tendencies to action ought to be inculcated.

Much of the book is based on the findings of contemporary psychology. For though common sense goes a long way in this dimension of life, one cannot deny that a half century of industrious research and observation by psychologists serves to confirm some parts of our "common sense," to refute other parts, and to go beyond it at many points. It would be folly, then, to ignore what psychologists have discovered.

Yet it must be admitted that it is often far from easy to find out *what* psychologists have discovered. What they claim is not difficult to ascertain, but to what extent these claims constitute *discoveries* is often far from clear. The field is rife with conflicting theories. There is much dispute as to the relevant variables. And by anyone's lights, much remains unknown. In such a situation there is nothing else to do but cut one's own path through the thickets of observation and experiment, indicating "where one is coming from," what seems to be the quality of the evidence at various points, and where ignorance remains.

A large amount of research which could have been discussed is not dealt with because of space limitations. To those who wish the author had gone further into the implications of his

---

*Henry J. Triezenberg, *et al.*, *Principles to Practice* (Grand Rapids, Mich.: Christian Schools International, 1979), p. 2.

conclusions for the schools, he must in honesty confess that he does not perceive with full clarity what those implications are. What is clear is that we must recognize not just curriculum but the whole school situation, and all those who work within it, as the educational agent for tendency learning. In this way, too, the relevance of what follows for parents and church school personnel becomes obvious.

Nicholas P. Wolterstorff, Ph.D.　　Henry J. Triezenberg, Ph.D.
Policy Consultant　　　　　　　*Curriculum Administrator*

Acknowledgments

Dr. Wolterstorff is currently a fellow at the Calvin Center for Christian Scholarship. For most of the time that he was writing this book, he was chairman of the Philosophy Department at Calvin College and a curriculum policy consultant for the National Union of Christian Schools, now Christian Schools International. The need for this study became apparent, and its development proceeded, in discussions with fellow policy consultants, especially Wilson Haarsma, William Hendricks, Kay Hoitenga, and Dr. Donald Oppewal. Drs. Martin Bolt and Mary Vander Goot of the Calvin College Psychology Department critically read the manuscript and offered especially helpful suggestions. Klaaske deGroot-deKoning and Sandy Vander Zicht of Christian Schools International, and Marlin Van Elderen of Eerdmans edited the manuscript. Many other people read this essay in manuscript form and offered constructive suggestions and criticisms. To all of them, our sincere thanks.

Credits

PART ONE:

The Context
of
Tendency Learning

1

Tendency Learning

Those who teach do so with a variety of aims. For the purpose of our discussion in this book we shall be concentrating on only one of these: the aim of producing, or occasioning, desired changes in the persons being taught. In turn, from among the many types of changes at which the teacher may aim, we shall consider only three, again making no claims as to the comprehensiveness of our classification.

One type of alteration a teacher will characteristically seek is an increase in the student's awareness of *what is true*. The change being sought is one from ignorance to knowledge, or from a false belief—or no belief—about something to a true belief. We might call learning which consists in acquiring a true belief about something *cognitive* (or intellectual) learning. A teacher may seek to help a student acquire the knowledge that the key of A major has three sharps, F#, C#, and G#; or that a basketball player in possession of the ball may move only if he or she continuously bounces the ball with one hand; or that certain familiar letters of the alphabet are pronounced differently when they appear in German words from the way they usually sound in English words.

A second type of change promoted by a person who is teaching someone else may be an increase in *ability* or capability, competence or skill. This type of learning we might call *ability* learning. To use our three examples, a piano instructor will seek to help a student acquire the ability to play the A-major scale smoothly, making certain that the appropriate fingers fall on the correct black and white keys; or a coach will drill the members of the basketball team until they are able to control the ball and their movements; or a German teacher will show the student how holding the lips and tongue in certain ways can enable one to produce sounds not normally heard in English. Many of our abilities are acquired by learning, though not all of them are: some we simply acquire in the course of maturing as human beings.

Third, those who teach characteristically aim at altering the *inclinations* or dispositions of their students to act in certain ways in various types of situations. The increase or decrease of some inclination or disposition as the result of a learning or training process may be called *tendency* learning. The piano instructor wants the student to be disposed to sharp the F's and C's and G's when playing a piece in the key of A major; the basketball coach wants the guard to be inclined to dribble the ball on the court without being called for a traveling violation; the German teacher wants the student reading a lesson aloud to have the tendency to pronounce the words as nearly as possible to the way a student in Germany would. The situations for which the teacher is attempting to alter the students' tendencies may sometimes be classroom situations, but most often they will be situations of the sort to be found both inside and outside the classroom.

Obviously abilities and tendencies are closely related; but they are not the same. Having a tendency to do something presupposes having the ability to do it; but one may well have the ability to do something while having the tendency to do it in only the rarest of situations—for example, where earning a passing grade in a course depends on it. Tendencies are grounded in desires, wishes, commitments, values, and the like. Abilities involve no such dispositions.

Some of our tendencies are habits. Indeed, a good deal of teaching aims at inculcating habits in the student. The teacher wants the student to manifest certain tendencies not by conscious choice but as a matter of habit. Clearly no one ever became an accomplished pianist or basketball player or speaker of German without having a large number of the sorts of tendency that we mentioned in our examples above become matters of habit. But not all of our tendencies are habits. Some of them involve the tendency to *decide* in certain characteristic ways.

My question in this essay is: What are the responsible and effective strategies for altering the tendencies of persons? In exploring this, we shall not be ignoring cognitive learning and ability learning, for beliefs, abilities, and tendencies, though distinct, are interdependent phenomena. In our lives the pursuit of any one of these is always intertwined with the presence and pursuit of the other two.

Tendency learning has become a matter for intense study, concern, and even controversy among educators. One of the principal manifestations of this is widespread discussion on the nature of *moral education*. While many would agree that there is more to moral education than cultivating certain tendencies, almost no one would deny that there is no moral education *without* the cultivation of tendencies.

What accounts for this rise of interest in moral education and, more generally, in tendency learning? I think it is the result of two developments in our society. The first is a breakdown in the consensus about how human beings should live and act, and the replacement of that consensus with a pluralism of differing views. All around us the question is being asked with urgency: *Which* tendencies shall we cultivate in our students? No longer can we fall back on the unity of earlier societies, in which nearly everyone agreed on the fundamental tendencies to be cultivated in their children, so that there was little conscious reflection on the matter.

Second, over the past half century a great deal of psychological inquiry and theorizing has focused on how tendencies are cultivated in people. But the result of all this scientific activity has in the main not been consensus but controversy and conflict. Even where there has been consensus on what tendencies ought to be cultivated in children, there is little agreement on how to do so. Common sense and tradition have been dislodged from their positions of eminence, but nothing has yet emerged to take their place.

The aim of altering the tendencies of students is, I said, characteristic of teachers. From this it does not automatically follow, of course, that it is *justified*. Indeed, some of those participating in the current controversies concerning tendency learning contend that it is in fact immoral for teachers to seek to alter the tendencies of their students. Some say that the teacher not only should *not aim* to influence students' tendencies but should consciously *seek to avoid* doing so. Set the students on the road to knowledge, cultivate in them certain abilities, but let the students themselves freely decide what they will do with this knowledge and these abilities—that is the contention.

An odor of sterile academicism surrounds such discussions. As will become obvious in the course of our examination, it is virtually impossible for a teacher to avoid seeking to shape students' tendencies—to strengthen some and weaken others—and it is certainly impossible for a teacher to act in such a way that he or she will *in fact* not alter the students' tendencies. To reject one educational practice in favor of another is inevitably to choose a line of action which has one set of effects on a student's tendencies rather than another. And so the responsible and perceptive teacher will make choices in the light of these effects, thus aiming at one set of effects rather than another, rather than vainly seeking to have no effect. *Which* tendencies to seek to inculcate, and *how*, are the relevant questions—not *whether*.

2

Teaching Responsibility

Even if it were not inevitable that teachers aim at shaping the tendencies of their students, tendency goals would, it seems to me, be dominant among those who seek to impart a *Christian* education. Let me elaborate on this by way of a brief sketch of the rudiments of a philosophy of Christian education.

Every philosophy of education grows out of an image of man in the world. So we must begin by looking at some of the main features of the Christian vision of life and reality. At its foundation is the conviction that this world in which we live and to which we belong is a *creation*. It is not something sufficient unto itself. It points beyond itself to God who brought it into existence. And the world he brought into existence is ordered and structured, a *cosmos*, as the Greeks called it, a world of laws and things satisfying those laws.

Time was when it would have been necessary at this point in the discussion to emphasize humanity's embeddedness in the physical creation. We human beings are earthlings among earthlings, sisters to the birds of the air and brothers to the beasts of the field. That scarcely needs to be said in our secular age. What must be stressed today is that man is the crown of the physical creation. In human beings the bond between God and his creation finds its focus.

What is the essence of this crowning status? The core of our uniqueness among earthlings is that human beings and human beings alone are responsible. They and they alone have duties, obligations. They and they alone are capable of guilt, for to be guilty is to violate one's responsibilities. Christians do not see these responsibilities as free-floating. They see them all as given by God. Humanity alone God has *graced* with responsibilities. He does so by holding us responsible—answerable, accountable—to himself.

God requires of his human creatures that we obey certain laws which specify our responsibilities. In its depth all human responsibility is responsibility to God, and all defection from responsibility is at its root letting God down. The depth dimension of all human responsibility is that it is a relation of persons to Person which leaps out of the created order of things. Through human beings, God's creation is bound to its Maker by cords of responsibility.

Here we cannot discuss the full texture of what we are responsible to God for doing. But over against the all-too-common assumption that our responsibilities to God comprise nothing more than our responsibilities for acting in certain ways with respect to him—honoring and trusting and worshiping him—it is worth emphasizing some other factors.

We have responsibilities for acting in certain ways with respect to human beings. These, too, are responsibilities to God. We are responsible *to* God *for* loving our neighbor as ourselves. This presupposes of course that we are to love ourselves. To despise yourself, to long to be what you cannot be and so to neglect becoming what you can become, to squander your life instead of nourishing your potential—all these are ways to fail in your responsibility to God. All of us are to seek our own fulfilment but equally to exhibit solidarity with others, to stand in their stead, to love them as ourselves, to seek their fulfilment as we seek our own. Indeed, in seeking the other's fulfilment we will find our own.

We also have responsibilities to God for acting in certain ways with respect to the physical creation around us. We are to subdue it, to tame it, to order it, to humanize it, though in the manner of a gardener, not a bulldozer. With respect to the animals, more specifically, we are to rule over them, to be masters over them. We are to rule over "all the beasts of the earth and all the birds of the air and all the creatures that move on the ground" (Gen. 1:30).

An older Protestant tradition rightly heard in such Old Testament passages God's injunction not just to engage in agriculture and animal husbandry but to humanize the whole of creation by our labor, thus to develop culture. So this tradition spoke of a "cultural mandate." Labor which humanizes God's creation and brings forth human culture is obedience to God the Creator.

It is especially in the authorization and injunction to have dominion that the songwriter of old Israel saw man's crowning status among fellow earthlings. You have crowned man with glory and honor, he says to God. And then at once he goes on, "You made him ruler over the works of your hands; you put everything under his feet" (Ps. 8:5–6). This ruling status is a key component in our being made in the image of God, as the biblical writers conceived it. With characteristic Hebrew parallelism the writer of Genesis says:

> Then God said, "Let us make man in our image, in our likeness, and let them rule over the fish of the sea and the birds of the air, . . . over all the earth, and over all the creatures that move along the ground" (Gen. 1:26).

There is, in summary, a triplicate pattern to what we are responsible *to* God *for* doing. We are responsible to God for how we act with respect to God. We are responsible to God for how we act with respect to ourselves and our fellow human beings. We are responsible to God for how we act with respect to nature.

We cannot leave this brief discussion concerning our status as responsible creatures without sounding one more note. Human responsibility, I have been saying, consists in God's holding us responsible to himself for acting in certain ways—that is, for obeying certain rules, certain normative laws. The normative laws which specify our responsibilities have the status of being God's will for human action, his rule for human life. That is the Christian vision. But the Christian adds at once that they are the will, the command, of a *loving* God. And because they are the will of a loving God, our joy and fulfilment lie in carrying out our responsibilities. What God wants is that we should each live responsibly, and thus joyfully, before him, in the world, among our fellow humans, with ourselves.

We have spoken thus far of creation. The next chapter in the Christian story is the fall. In freedom man revolted against God and refused to live in trustful obedience, preferring instead to act as if he were self-normed. Thereupon he became confused about his responsibilities and defected from them. He mutilated the earth. He victimized his fellows. He squandered his abilities. He set up surrogate gods. A dark cloud fell over creation, so that the whole of it groans for deliverance, as Paul says (Rom. 8:22).

Now comes the third chapter in the Christian story—so difficult for us to believe, yet so finely tuned to our deepest hopes. God resolved not to leave his creation in the grip of its misery but to act instead for its renewal. Out of love he acts so that human beings can once again live in joyful fulfilment with themselves, their neighbors, nature, and God. There is a drift, a direction, in history. In spite of all the manifestations of evil which we see around us, all the perversity and suffering, Christians are nonetheless persuaded that history as a whole, in all its ups and downs, is "arrowed" toward the ultimate renewal of creation.

No doubt, as the hymnwriter puts it, "God moves in a mysterious way, His wonders to perform." Yet God's motions are by no means entirely mysterious. For at the heart of God's strategy for renewal is his calling out of human beings, to whom he says that he will be their God if they will be obedient agents in his cause. God has chosen to work in such a way that he needs his human creatures in order to accomplish his purposes.

God's call came first to Israel—a particular nation from among the nations. Then it came in decisive fashion to his own Son Jesus Christ. And from Pentecost onward the call comes to all human beings everywhere. It is a call to repent, to believe, to follow in the footsteps of his Son Jesus Christ and to be his disciples. The band of those who accept this call to become agents in God's cause of renewal constitutes the church. Thus at Pentecost a new people was given birth, a transnational people, which, while it transcends all nations, is now also to be found within each. "Elect from every nation, Yet one o'er all the earth."

We may distinguish four tasks in what God asks of those who answer his call to repent, believe, follow his Son, and become agents in his cause of renewal. In the first place, the church is called to *bear witness* to what is to be seen with eyes and heard with ears—namely, God's mighty deeds in the cause of renewal.

Peter made this clear in the first Christian sermon:

> "Men of Israel, listen to this: Jesus of Nazareth was a man accredited by God to you by miracles, wonders and signs, which God did among you through him, as you yourselves know. This man was handed over to you by God's set purpose and foreknowledge; and you, with the help of wicked men, put him to death by nailing him to the cross. But God raised him from the dead, freeing him from the agony of death, because it was impossible for death to keep its hold on him" (Acts 2:22–24).

Second, the church is called to *serve* all human beings everywhere, working and praying for healing, liberation, and fulfilment in all of life—in politics, in science, in social structures, in technology, in art, in recreation—willingly undergoing sacrifice and suffering when necessary. The church does not have the option of remaining passive in the face of deprivation and oppression and distortion. As Christ the Lord of the church took on the form of a servant, so the church is called to be a serving, ministering presence in the world, aiding the victims of structures that deprive and oppress, laboring to abolish such structures, seeking to replace them with structures in which persons find fulfilment.

A third calling of the church is to *give evidence* in its own style of life of the new life to be found in Jesus Christ. The church is called to be a paradigm, an exemplary community in its work, in its worship, in its fellowship. Its own life is to demonstrate the firstfruits of the full harvest, the signposts of the kingdom. The church is not merely to wait with grim patience for the new age when the Spirit will fully renew all existence. It must already, here and now, manifest signs of that renewing Spirit.

Finally, the church is called to *disciple* all people, urging them to repent and believe and join the band of Christ's followers, thus to share in the work of being witness, servant, and evidence.

As the band of Christ's followers, the church is an alien presence within every nation. Called and committed to be God's agent for the coming of his kingdom in a fallen and resistant world, to serve as the revolutionary vanguard of society ushering in a new order, the church finds itself ever in tension with those who want to hang on to the present order. The new community of the church, in which the Christian finds fundamental identity, is an *alternative* society.

One more point before we consider how this vision applies to education. Crucial to the character of the church is the fact that it has certain sacred writings, namely, the books of the Old and New Testaments. These Scriptures are the expression of the religion of ancient persons and peoples, but more importantly they are acknowledged by the church as authoritative guides for the thought and life of Christians in this present age. Becoming a member of the church involves submitting oneself to their authority.

These Scriptures are taken as authoritative guides because Christians are persuaded that it is integral to God's mode of working for human renewal to *speak to* his human creatures. In the Bible we find an authoritative record of some of what God said to ancient persons and peoples; and by way of those ancient words we hear God speaking to us today. True, God's speech to us today is not confined to the Bible, but what he says there is the touchstone, the criterion, for what he says to us in other modes and manners. Convinced of this, the Christian community acknowledges the Bible as authoritative for life and thought.

Of course the Bible does not offer specific counsel for every concrete situation that we face. It gives guidelines, paradigm situations, advice by way of example. Essential to maturing in the faith is learning how to get from that to one's own concrete situation. Often there are disagreements on such matters in the community; just as often there is consensus.

Thus the Bible occupies a central position in the Christian's answer to the question, How do we discover our responsibilities? For one thing, even though the Bible is not a political or economic or aesthetic or even moral handbook, it does contain a wealth of guidance, often quite specific, not only about what God asks of his redeemed people, but also about what he asks of his human creatures generally. But secondly, the Bible serves to open our eyes to creation and its normative structure—to what God asks of us by virtue of our status as created human beings— so that we can go on to inquire on our own. Where once we may have thought of aesthetic values and artistic goals along Platonic or Romantic-humanist or Marxist lines, the Bible opens our eyes to how those are distorted visions of God's will for art in human life. From there on we act like grown-up human beings, thinking things through for ourselves, not demanding a biblical word on all the details of human responsibility.

In spite of the centrality of the Bible in the Christian's apprehension of our human responsibility, we must nonetheless resist the delusion that Christians alone discern what human beings are responsible for doing. People in many cultures have enunciated it as a fundamental principle of morality that we are to treat others as we would like them to treat us. Though not identical with the biblical principle to love one's neighbor as oneself, that is at least an approximation to it.

Now we can move on to education. Like any other community with a cause and lifestyle of its own, the church finds it necessary to educate, not only its new recruits, but also its longtime members. Thus education by and for the community comes into existence, conducted informally by parents, conducted formally by teachers and pastors. And that, at its most basic, is Christian education: education *by* the Christian community *for* the Christian community.

To put it that way sounds inward-looking—and so, in a certain sense, it is. But we have seen that the church exists not for its own sake but for the sake of God's cause in the world. That cause is the overcoming of alienation from God and liberation from the oppression, deprivation, and suffering in which sin works itself out, so that human beings may dwell in God's *shalom*, where there is harmony and delight in all dimensions of existence. The Christian is one who follows Jesus Christ, who was, in Bonhoeffer's phrase, the "Man for others." And so, in being education for the Christian community, Christian education is education for the sake of all.

It used to be said, particularly in the Calvinist tradition, that the goal of Christian education is to impart to the student the Christian "world and life view." The intent behind putting it this way was to affirm that the gospel pertains to all of life and not just to some "religious" part. But this formulation is inadequate, for it puts too much emphasis on a "view," that is, on what we have called cognition. To be identified with the people of God and to share in its work does indeed require that one have a system of belief—call it "the Christian world and life view." But it requires more than that. It requires the Christian *way of life*. Christian education is education aimed at training for the Christian way of life, not just education aimed at inculcating the Christian world and life view.

This implies, straightforwardly, that what we have called tendency learning is an essential component in a program of Christian education. Christian education points to a certain way of living and acting—one in which a person lives and acts responsibly, in obedience to God's will, as an agent of God's cause in the world.[1] To act responsibly in the world obviously requires *knowledge* of the world and of God's normative laws for one's actions. Likewise it requires *abilities* of various sorts. So a program of Christian education will include among its goals both cognitive learning and ability learning. But if it were to stop there, its fundamental goal would not yet have been achieved. One can have the knowledge and the abilities required for acting responsibly and yet have no tendency to engage in such action. A program of Christian education will take that further step of cultivating the appropriate *tendencies* in the child. It will have tendency learning as one of its fundamental goals.

Let me put these points in a slightly different way. The ultimate goal of *all* education, as Christians see it, is that those who are taught shall live in such a way as to carry out their responsibilities to God and find joy and delight in so doing. The Christian parent and teacher seeks to do what he or she thinks all parents and teachers should seek to do. A philosophy of education which has this as the proper ultimate goal of education may be called a *responsibility theory of education*. Notice that a person need not be a Christian to hold a responsibility theory of education. A Jew or Muslim might also believe that the proper goal of education is that the student shall so live as to carry out his or her responsibilities to God, but disagree with the Christian about the

---

[1]When I speak of "action," I do not mean to exclude contemplation and meditation. These are themselves actions—actions far too seldom practiced in the contemporary West.

location and nature of God's redemptive action in history, and consequently about the details of our responsibilities. But if there may be responsibility theories of education which are not *Christian*, I have tried to show that a Christian philosophy of education—and, more specifically, a philosophy of Christian education—will be a responsibility theory.

Anyone who holds a responsibility theory of education will include cognitive goals among the aims of the educator. If we are to act responsibly we must be in tune with reality. We must have knowledge of how things are. We must know the relevant facts along with the relevant norms. So one of the goals of education will be to impart to the student knowledge of how things are. Teaching will aim at cognitive learning, at producing an increase in the students' knowledge.

If we are to act responsibly we must, in the second place, have abilities (capabilities, competences, skills) in a large number of different areas. We must have the ability ourselves to acquire knowledge, and we must have the ability to discern what we ought to do in a variety of situations. We must have the ability to read, the ability to perform arithmetical computations. Education, accordingly, will have goals concerning abilities. It will aim to produce an increase in the students' abilities. It will aim at ability learning.

But if responsible action is to ensue, more is necessary than for the students to have knowledge of the relevant matters and the ability to perform the relevant actions. Knowledge and ability are not yet performance. It is also necessary that the students' tendencies, ranging all the way from their unreflective habits to highly self-conscious commitments, be those of acting in accord with the normative laws for right action. Education, accordingly, must have among its goals to secure—always in morally defensible ways—the formation of right tendencies. It must seek to develop in students the habit of speaking their native language correctly. It must seek to develop in students a commitment to the principle of doing what is honest. Education must aim at producing alterations in what students tend (are disposed, are inclined) to do. It must aim at tendency learning.

3

Rival Educational Theories

Our discussion of strategies for tendency learning will be set within the context of a responsibility type of educational theory. One does not find many examples of this type of theory today. Contemporary educators are extremely chary of seeing education as aimed at responsible action, let alone as aimed at students' carrying out their responsibilities to God. They would much rather think of education as aimed at growth or socialization or something of that sort.

In order to outline more clearly the main contours of a responsibility type of educational theory, so that the point of what follows will be evident despite the unfamiliarity of this sort of theory, let us contrast the responsibility type of theory with some of its major alternatives. For to understand a theory, it often helps to see what theories it opposes. I shall identify and briefly analyze what seem to me the three dominant contemporary alternatives to the responsibility type of theory. So dominant are these three that, in my judgment, almost all *fundamental* disputes about the goals of education among educators today are disputes among representatives of these three broad types of educational theory. There are other ways to classify contemporary theories of education, of course, but for our present purpose this seems most illuminating.

MATURATIONAL TYPE

One prominent type of educational theory I shall call the maturational type. Such a theory is one which holds that the goal of the educational process is the mental health and happiness of the child, and that this happens when the individual's innate desires, interests, and motivations are satisfied. The business of the school, then, is to contribute in whatever way relevant to the attainment of such satisfaction. Examples of educational theorists who hold maturationist views are A. S. Neill, Carl Rogers, and Raths & Simon.

One almost always finds the image of biological growth in the exposition of such theories. The function of the school, says the maturationist, is to provide nourishment for the maturing child. The core idea is that children will turn out best if they are allowed to grow without inhibition in a nourishing environment. One hears talk of the need for providing "growth experiences" to students, and it is the prominence of the image of biological growth in the exposition of these theories that leads me to call them *maturational* theories.

Of course, no educator is for immaturity. All are in favor of the students' becoming mature. In that broad sense, then, all theories of education are maturational theories. But not all educators by any means understand maturation in the same way as the person whom I am calling a maturationist; accordingly, not everyone holds that the entire business of the school is to contribute to the satisfaction of the student's innate impulses.

At the heart of the maturational type of theory are a specific concept of the self and an insistence that it is important for each self to express or realize itself. The fundamental theses are that each *self* comes with a variety of innate desires, interests, and motivations, that mental health and happiness will be achieved if these innate desires are allowed to find their satisfaction within the natural and social environment, and that an individual's mental health and happiness constitute his or her ultimate good. Maturationists characteristically stress the malleability of the natural and social environments. All of them would agree that these are not totally malleable and that the individual has some innate desires which cannot possibly be satisfied without ensuing pain. But maturationists hold that no fundamental unhappiness and mental disease result from allowing these particular innate desires and interests to be extinguished by the unalterable features of our natural and social environments. What must be avoided at all costs, though, is imposing the wishes and expectations of others onto the self. Down that road lie unhappiness and disease. The way to that ultimate good which is personal health and happiness is self-expression, not the internalization of others' wishes.

The proper goal of the educator, then, is to provide the child with an environment which is *permissive*—in that there is no attempt to impose the wishes of others onto the child—and *nourishing*—in that it provides for the satisfaction of the child's desires and interests. On this all maturationists would agree. Some of them would say that this is the limit of what the school should do. It should confine itself to providing a permissive nourishing environment in which children can express themselves. Others, however, argue that persons characteristically develop internal blockages or inhibitions of their natural desires and interests, with the result that they fall into mental disease and unhappiness. These maturationists would contend that the school should not only provide a permissive nourishing environment, but also work to remove inhibitions on self-expression.

It may be well at this point to allow a representative of this point of view to speak for himself. I quote from the prominent American psychologist of the late nineteenth and early twentieth centuries, G. Stanley Hall:

> The guardians of the young should strive first to keep out of nature's way and to prevent harm and should merit the proud title of the defenders of the happiness and rights of children. They should feel profoundly that childhood, as it comes from the hand of God, is not corrupt but illustrates the survival of the most consummate thing in the world; they should be convinced that there is nothing else so worthy of love, reverence and service as the body and soul of the growing child.
>
> Before we let the pedagog loose upon childhood, we must overcome the fetishes of the alphabet, of the multiplication tables, and must reflect that but a few generations ago the ancestors of all of us were illiterate. There are many who ought not be educated and who would be better in mind, body and morals if they knew no school. What shall it profit a child to gain the world of knowledge and lose his own health?[1]

It is easy to see why those holding a maturational view often speak of the properly run school as "child-centered."

[1]G. Stanley Hall, "The Ideal School Based on Child Study," in *The Forum*, 32 (1901), p. 24.

Anti-maturationists counter this slogan by claiming that one might as well call the properly run school "subject-centered," since one never teaches some person without teaching some *thing*. But that misses the point. The maturationist holds that the desires and interests of the child *ought to determine the subject-matter*.

Maturationists hold not only that persons come with in-built sets of desires and interests, but also that these change over time. The interests and desires of an adolescent are different from those of an adult. Many would say that these changes come in innately pre-programmed, relatively well-integrated stages. There is Gesell's three-year-old "No"-saying stage, Erikson's adolescent identity-crisis stage, and so on. Maturationists who accept such stage theories naturally hold as a corollary that an environment which conduces to the mental health of persons in one stage may not conduce to the mental health of those in another stage.

The first important thinker to articulate a maturational theory was Rousseau. Later it was to become the view of the Romantics. By now maturational thinking pervades not only North American education, with its open classrooms, its discovery techniques, its values-clarification strategies, its de-schooling proposals, and its stress on self-expression, but it also pervades therapeutic psychology, with its sensitivity sessions, its "Rogerian" therapy, and the like.[2] What these educators and therapists alike seek to promote is the individual's happiness and mental health. Their fundamental thesis is that mental health will be secured if and only if persons are allowed to express themselves. Remove inhibitions, allow each person to "do his or her own thing," nurture personal growth—these have become the rallying cries.

The normative theory underlying the maturationist view is always antinomianism or ethical egoism. On the antinomian view, the categories of *right* and *wrong* are said to have no application, so that they ought to be discarded. Ethical egoists argue that what is right for a given person just consists of what satisfies his or her own desires and interests, so that the self is its own norm.

---

[2] For an extensive critique of such theories and fads see Paul C. Vitz, *Psychology as Religion: The Cult of Self-Worship* (Eerdmans, 1977).

Either way, we hear regularly that we should avoid blaming and praising others for their actions. Blame and praise tend to cause the person whose actions are being evaluated to internalize the evaluations of the evaluator, and this is precisely what must be avoided at all costs. That is the prime evil. If the maturationists had their way, praising and blaming other persons for their actions would disappear from human life.

This is not to deny that the maturational strand of thought has made an important contribution to human culture. To the maturationists we owe our awareness that children have an inner developing self and the discovery that the character of the adult can be traced to the self of the child. It is to them we owe our realization that the child is a person in his or her own right, not just some object waiting to become a person upon entering adulthood.

Yet it will be obvious that the maturational view conflicts directly with the Christian view of life and reality. For the Christian believes that there are indeed normative laws for action. And what those laws require of us is obedience to our Creator, rather than expression of ourselves. Certainly such obedience incorporates an authentic love of self, but it also incorporates self-giving service to one's fellow human beings, the tender cherishing of the nature within which we live, and thankful acknowledgment of God's action in creation and redemption.

If the self always and only desired what God requires, the relevance of these points would be purely theoretical. But that is most emphatically not the case. We are all divided selves. Within us there is indeed the impulse to find our rest in God the Creator and to serve our fellows, but there is also the impulse to pride and self-aggrandizing disobedience. Thus, some of our impulses must be suppressed, others satisfied. The sorting-out which this demands requires a criterion outside the self and its desires.

SOCIALIZATION TYPE

A second broad type of current educational theory is what I shall call the *socialization type*. Socialization theorists say that the ultimate goal of the educational process is to "socialize" children. By this they mean inducting them into their society and making them well-functioning, contributing members of it. Children must be imprinted with the rules and roles and expectations of the surrounding society. Whereas the focus in maturational theories is on the *child*, the focus here is on *society*. Education is society's way of maintaining and perpetuating itself as a well-functioning organism. Emile Durkheim and B. F. Skinner are good examples of socialization theorists.

When we look at those groupings of people which are typically regarded as societies, we discover a massive commonality in beliefs, emotions, and behavior. They share ideals and rituals and objects of veneration (whether persons, places, events, or artifacts). They share understandings of their group's history and significance. They share practices and institutions and often religion and theology. What stamps someone as an American, for example, and not a Frenchman is this type of sharing with other Americans, not one's having been born in the United States or being a naturalized citizen of it. To be fully American is to venerate Lincoln and not Napoleon, to celebrate Independence Day and not Bastille Day, to prefer potato chips to croissants. Given the comprehensive goal of inducting children into such a society and making them well-functioning members of it, the socialization theorist believes that education must get children to adopt as their own the shared cognitive, emotional, and behavioral features of their society. The goal of education, as the socialization theorist often puts it, is for children to internalize these shared social phenomena.

But there is more than this to socializing children. Not only are children to become good Canadians or good Germans or whatever, they are also to *contribute* to making Canada good or Germany good, etc. They are to play constructive *roles* in their society. In every society we can discern a unique and highly articulate structure of social roles and role-expectations. The socialization theorist holds that the educator must acquaint children with these various role-expectations and equip them to "play" a particular set of roles. To equip me for "my station and its duties"—that is the goal. Thus the concept of a social role and its duties characteristically plays a large part in the thought of socialization theorists.

Naturally socialization theorists will want to find a good fit between the student and the role for which he or she is being prepared. Usually, though, they assume that children are highly malleable. With suitable training each child can be made to fit a wide variety of different social roles. But this will not happen if children are just allowed to "flower." Some of their behavior must be quenched, others kindled. They must be disciplined. Whereas *freedom* was a central concept for the maturationist, *discipline* occupies a central position in the thought of the socialization theorists.

One of the most profound of all modern socialization theorists was the French sociologist Emile Durkheim (1858–1917). It will be helpful to look briefly at how Durkheim fleshed out the socialization ideology in his book *Moral Education*.[3] Durkheim was convinced that the most crucial issue facing modern society is that of working out a secular morality. Since morality, on his view, always involves authority, he was led to ask what is available in the secular vision to replace the ultimate authority of God. His answer was: society. The group, he says, "is the sacred thing, par excellence" (p. 82). "Each [member of the group] shares the religious deference inspired by this ideal" (p. 82).

Durkheim's application of this vision to education comes through with particular clarity in these passages:

> True education begins only when the moral and intellectual culture acquired by man has become complex and plays too important a part in the whole of the common life to leave its transmission from one generation to the next to the hazards of circumstance. Hence, the elders feel the need to intervene, to bring about themselves the transmission of culture by epitomizing their experiences and deliberately passing on ideas, sentiments, and knowledge from their minds to those of the young (p. 189).

> The school has, above all, the function of linking the child to this society. As for the family, it itself suffices to arouse and sustain in the hearts of its members those sentiments necessary for its existence. On the contrary,

[3]Page references in the text are to the translation by E. K. Wilson and H. Schnurer (The Free Press, 1973).

as for the nation—as here understood—the school is the only moral agent through which the child is able systematically to learn to know and love his country. It is precisely this fact that lends pre-eminent significance to the part played by the school today in the shaping of national morality (p. 79).

[The teacher] is an instrument of a great moral reality which surpasses him and with which he communicates more directly than does the child, since it is through his intermediation that the child communicates with it. Just as the priest is the interpreter of God, he is the interpreter of the great moral ideas of his time and country. Whatever is linked with these ideas, whatever the significance and authority attributed to them, necessarily spreads to him and everything coming from him since he expresses these things and embodies them in the eyes of children. In this authority, which derives from a quite impersonal source, nothing of arrogance, vanity, or pedantry must enter. It is entirely brought about through the teacher's respect for his role or, if one may put it this way, for his ministry (p. 155).

The way of developing the child morally is not to repeat to him, with however much emotion and conviction, a certain number of very general maxims valid eternally and everywhere, but to make him understand his country and his times; to make him feel his responsibilities, to initiate him into life and thus to prepare him to take his part in the collective tasks awaiting him (pp. 123f.).[4]

---

[4] E. K. Wilson summarizes Durkheim's view well: "For him, education is above all a social means to a social end—the means by which a society guarantees its own survival. The teacher is society's agent, the critical link in cultural transmission. It is his task to create a social, a moral, being. Through him, society creates man in his image. 'That,' says Durkheim, 'is the task and the glory of education. It is not merely a matter of allowing an individual to develop in accordance with his nature, disclosing whatever hidden capacities lie there only waiting to be revealed. *Education creates a new being*'" (p. xiv). It is interesting that Wilson goes on to describe these views as "aspects of a conception of education that differs dramatically from that which apparently prevails among Americans. For us, education is much more child-centered, an individual matter, an enterprise dedicated, as the stock phrase puts it, to the maximum development of the individual personality. The adaptation of curriculum, personnel, and facilities to the needs of the individual child—this is the great good in the pantheon of pedagogical virtues" (p. xiii).

In response one wants to protest: Surely one's society can be *wrong* on some matters. But how then can it be regarded as the sacred moral reality? And if it cannot be so regarded, then it cannot be the ultimate goal of education to *induct* the child into his or her society. The child must be given some standard of critique on that society.

Admittedly Durkheim does now and then supplement what was quoted above with claims like this:

> There is one association that among all the others enjoys a genuine preeminence and that represents the end, par excellence, of moral conduct. This is the political society, i.e., the nation—but the nation conceived of as a partial embodiment of the idea of humanity.

> The nation, as it lays claim to the contemporary conscience, is not the inflated and jealous state that knows no rules other than those directed toward its own interest and that deems itself emancipated from all the discipline of morality. What gives the nation its moral value is that it most closely approximates the society of mankind, at present unrealized in fact and perhaps unrealizable, yet representing the limiting case, or the ideal limit toward which we always strive (pp. 80f.).

Unfortunately, Durkheim offers no suggestion as to what constitutes "the idea of humanity," no criterion for deciding when one must depart from the standards of one's own society, no hint as to what we should replace those standards with once we depart from them. And so these references to humanity and mankind do not function in the structure of Durkheim's thought. What he explicitly says is that "if a society is the end of morality, it is also its producer" (p. 86). Perhaps what he has in mind is that societies, to some extent, provide us with principles of critique on their own actions. Although Great Britain fails to live up to its own ideals, it is with British *ideals* that British children must be inspired and imbued. They must be told, "Look at what Britain says, not at what it does."

In short, Durkheim is a cultural relativist. This is characteristic of socialization theorists in general: they regard the normative laws holding for the members of one society as distinct from those holding for another. Customarily they explain this, as Durkheim does, by suggesting that moral norms are simply the creations of a society. They specify what a society thinks it is right to do. Moral norms are social rules.

At this point responsibility theorists, particularly Christians, will raise their most fundamental objection. The "sacred moral reality" is not determined by political or social boundaries. It is the same for all humanity—Canadians and Turks and Chinese and everyone else. It is God to whom all are called to act in obedience. Not only are the actions of a nation to be measured against its own ideals, but those ideals themselves must also be subjected to critique. Corruption and self-centeredness enter into the ideals of nations as well as into their actions.

This is no less true for the church of Jesus Christ. Someone might suggest that Christians should adopt the socialization type of theory as their own, modifying Durkheim only to the extent of taking the church as the normative social reality rather than the nation. But the ideals and actions of the church are not the norm for human existence. They too must be measured by something outside itself—the will of the Lord of the Church, the Creator and Redeemer of humanity.

In these brief comments on socialization theories I have focused on Durkheim because his articulation far outstrips any other in its depth and imagination. I might as well have culled statements expressing the traditional ideology of the public school. Over and over it has been said that the public school is the great instrument for passing on the nation's values and way of life, and that, accordingly, it is the fundamental instrument for securing national unity and continuity. A few passages from a pamphlet entitled *Moral and Spiritual Values in the Public Schools,* issued in 1951 by the Educational Policies Commission, demonstrate a socialization theory that is not so much asserted as taken for granted.

> It is important to ask whether a substantial agreement exists among the people of the United States concerning the moral and spiritual values by which they should live and which they wish to see embodied in the character and conduct of their children. . . . In spite of relapses and variations in practice, . . . there is a generally accepted

body of values which the American people tend to use as a compass for finding their way through political, social, economic, and personal issues. . . . It is these moral and spiritual values upon which the American people as a whole have agreed to manage their individual lives and their corporate activities, including their public schools.

INTERACTION-DEVELOPMENTAL TYPE

A third prominent type of educational theory I shall call the *interaction-developmental type*. It is represented especially by the Swiss Jean Piaget and the American Lawrence Kohlberg. Strictly speaking, this is a subtype of the maturational theory, but its prominence in recent years makes it worth singling out for special attention. On this view, the goal of education is not just to permit children to flower nor just to imprint them with the commonalities and roles of society, but to advance them in their patterns of reasoning toward the attainment of "cognitive equilibrium."

Human beings, so it is claimed, confront life and reality not with random thoughts but rather with integrated *patterns* of reasoning—about causality, about morality, and the like. These patterns are the common property of humanity. Nobody reasons in private, idiosyncratic patterns. However, people do proceed from one such integrated pattern of reasoning to another. They go through stages. They develop. Two persons may in fact be reasoning about morality with two quite different patterns. But that is not because they have their own private patterns. It is because they are in different stages.

As to the order of these stages, Piaget and Kohlberg affirm the following three fundamental laws:

1. The sequence of stages in our thinking about morality, causality, and the like is the same for all persons. Different persons move through the stages at different rates, and there are stages at which some persons never arrive. But everybody moves through the stages in the same order. Thus we can speak of earlier and later stages in general, without specifying *for whom*.

2. Nobody ever reverts to an earlier stage after having been in a later one.

3. Nobody ever skips a stage.

Why do people move from one stage to another? Piaget and Kohlberg repudiate some of the explanations for this which others might suspect. People do not move from one stage to another because of some innate programming which works itself out if they simply live long enough. Nor do they move because they have been *taught* the concepts belonging to a later stage. Nor do they move because they are subtly conditioned to do so or because they observe models in their environment operating at a higher stage. According to this theory, people move from one stage to the next because of a certain sort of interaction between their environment and the particular pattern of reasoning in which they find themselves. Development is the result of *interaction* between pattern and environment.

Specifically, Kohlberg and Piaget claim, everyone wants to eliminate "cognitive dissonance" (in other words, to attain "cognitive equilibrium"). This, they say, is what underlies stage advancement. Each successive stage in a particular hierarchy is "more highly differentiated" and "more thoroughly integrated" than its predecessors, and is thus better able to cope with experience. Experience confronts the later stage with less dissonance. Accordingly, when the dissonance between one's environment and stage of reasoning becomes sufficiently severe, one moves on to a higher stage in order to attain equilibrium. There the person rests, until that stage, too, yields an intolerable amount of dissonance in interaction with that part of the environment to which the concepts of that hierarchy apply.

What are the consequences of this theory for education? Piaget and Kohlberg argue that the ultimate goal of education is not to fill the child's mind with an assortment of items of knowledge but to advance the child from one stage of reasoning within a given hierarchy to another, from a less mature to a more mature stage. *Form (structure)*, not *content*, must be the focus of attention. The educator's main concern must not be *what* the child reasons about, but *how* the child reasons about it. This goal of advancing the student in the *form* of his or her reasoning is accomplished by producing dissonance between the environment of children and that particular stage within which they find themselves.

Later we shall look more closely at Kohlberg's theory of moral reasoning (pp. 79–100). Then we shall see how this general theory is articulated in one specific area and lodge some detailed criticisms of it. Here we shall make only a few general comments.

Obviously this particular educational ideology rests heavily on a network of psychological claims. And far from achieving consensus those claims remain highly controversial. But suppose the claims were true. What then should be said about this ideology?

Mainly what should be said is that it cannot possibly be a satisfactorily comprehensive ideology for education. I have argued that education should aim at responsible action and in fulfilling that goal should seek to shape the student's tendencies. But a striking feature of the interaction-developmental theory is that it concentrates wholly on *reasoning*, the *cognitive* side of education, and ignores the educator's calling to shape the student's tendencies. Or, to put it more accurately: the interaction-developmental theory focuses entirely on the child's *tendency to reason* in certain patterned ways. All other tendencies it ignores.

Ironically, its focus on the cognitive has struck many educators as the most attractive feature of the interaction-developmental view, particularly in moral education. Most research in this area has been conducted within a psychoanalytic framework or a behaviorist framework; and in both frameworks the cognitive was granted virtually no role whatever. So the rise of the interaction-developmental theory has seemed, for many, like a wave of liberation. Yet no program of education, certainly no program of Christian education, can be concerned solely with the student's practice of reasoning in certain ways.

Nor can a program of Christian education concern itself solely with the *form* of children's reasoning, leaving entirely to their judgment the application of this form. Kohlberg's principal reason for insisting, at least in the area of moral education, that teachers confine themselves to the children's *form* of reasoning, is that to give students guidance in how to apply a particular pattern of moral reasoning would be to infringe on the rights of students and parents. By contrast, if teachers concern themselves exclusively with stage advancement they will simply be promoting what comes naturally. But responsible Christian parents or teachers will not just be concerned that children reason about moral matters by using such concepts as *love* and *justice*. They will also be concerned to guide children in applying those concepts to the tangled thicket of our moral existence. That will be an essential component in educating for responsible action.

The claim that teachers who confine themselves to promoting stage advancement are only promoting what comes naturally lays bare the commitment of interaction-developmental theorists to the fundamental *goodness* of humanity. Discipline is no more a part of their outlook than it is of maturationists'. Both consider the whole business of the school to be promoting the growth, development, and maturation of the student. Differences between the two ideologies arise from differing views on how the "plants" are structured and how their flowering is to be nourished. Christians, by contrast, cannot blink their eyes to the fallenness of humanity. Some of our tendencies must be stifled.

We have looked at three broad contemporary alternatives to a responsibility theory of education, hoping to clarify the latter by contrast. Now we must move on to the central question of this essay: What are effective and responsible strategies for shaping a student's tendencies? What are effective and responsible strategies for tendency learning? That discussion will be set within the context of a responsibility theory of education.

PART TWO:

Strategies
for
Tendency Learning

4

The Structure of the Moral Agent

In the discussion that follows, I shall take our *moral* responsibilities to be our responsibilities for how we treat human beings. Given this understanding of "moral," it is clear from the foregoing that I do not regard the scope of human responsibilities as confined to those which are moral. We also have ecological responsibilities toward nature, religious responsibilities for actions with respect to God, as well as political, aesthetic, and intellectual responsibilities. None of these is to be reduced to moral responsibilities.

Nevertheless, from this whole terrain of education for responsible action it is moral education which has received by far the bulk of attention from psychologists. Accordingly, in what follows I shall focus first on moral education and at the end of the discussion in this part show how our conclusions can be generalized and applied to other areas. In this chapter I shall enter the topic of moral education by highlighting various facets of the moral agent. In succeeding chapters, these facets will be abstracted from that unified complex which is the moral agent, so that we can see what psychologists have to tell us about each of them. By a *moral agent*, I should note, I do not mean merely an agent *capable* of moral action but an agent who *does* in fact act morally. A moral agent is a virtuous person.

At the core of the moral agent lie certain tendencies to action. The moral agent is one who is disposed to act in certain ways—disposed to tell the truth, disposed to be of assistance to those who need aid, and so forth. In the most general terms, the moral agent is one who is disposed to act in accord with moral law.

But one needs more than a tendency to act in accord with moral law in order to rank as a moral agent. Everyone knows that people can be induced to have the tendency to act in certain regular ways by having the expectation of external rewards for acting that way or of external punishments for not acting that way built up in them. All would agree that a person is not a moral agent for acting in accord with moral law out of a desire to enjoy pleasant consequences or avoid unpleasant ones. In order to be a moral agent, the person's tendency to tell the truth, for example, must have been internalized, so that the tendency is sustained even without the expection of external reinforcement.

But if all we have is someone who has *internalized* certain tendencies to action, we still do not have a moral agent—even if those on the outside recognize these actions as being in accord with moral law. The agent must also learn to *evaluate actions morally* as right or wrong. This applies to the agent's own actions and those of others, those actually performed and those capable of being performed. To do that one must acquire the moral concepts of right and wrong and begin to learn how to apply them, that is, begin to learn which actions are right and which are wrong, thereby coming to adopt standards (principles) which are in accord with moral law.[1] If you tend to tell the truth and avoid lying, and if you have internalized this tendency, but you never judge these or any other actions as right or wrong, then you are not yet a moral agent. To be a moral agent one must acquire at least the basic elements of what may be called a *cognitive structure for morality*. This will include some moral concepts, convictions about how these concepts are to be applied in the form of acceptable standards, and reasons for those standards. On the Christian view these reasons will culminate in the ultimate moral law: Because you should love your neighbor as yourself.

But still something would be missing. I may tend to act in accord with moral law. That tendency may have been internalized in me. I may have a cognitive structure for morality enabling me correctly to judge the actions I tend to perform as being in accord with moral law. Yet on a given occasion I may perform an action which is in accord with moral law because I have figured

---

[1]These may be called moral standards, or principles. Thus by a moral standard (principle) I mean a correct belief as to what ought to be done in certain instances. To adopt a moral standard (principle) is to apprehend some facet of that total complex which is God's moral law.

out that doing so will somehow enable me to gain revenge on an enemy of mine. But if I perform what is—and what I recognize to be—a right action with an evil intention, I am not acting as a moral agent. We need to refine our definition to add that if one is to be a moral agent one must *act on* one's moral standards.

These are the essential components of the moral agent. At its basis are dispositions to act in accord with moral law; these dispositions have become internalized. But in addition to such dispositions the agent must have the beginnings of a correct cognitive structure for morality, on the principles of which he or she acts.

Few if any psychological studies of moral education acknowledge the full complexity of the moral agent as described above. And since most of them until recently have been conducted within a psychoanalytic or a behaviorist framework, almost all have neglected the essential role of cognition in the moral life. Yet in spite of the simplistic and reductionist character of the studies, several of them do illuminate one or another phase of moral education. So it is to the psychological studies that I now turn.[2]

In the next two chapters we shall look at what psychologists have to tell us about the inculcation of tendencies. Then we shall see what they have to tell us about the internalization of tendencies. In Chapter 8 we shall focus on what they have to tell us concerning the formation of a cognitive structure for morality *on which* one acts. In Chapter 9 we shall scrutinize a strategy for cultivating internalized tendencies to act in accord with the moral law which is largely ignored by the psychologists.

[2] A useful summary of the psychological studies concerning one phase of the moral life—acts of "altruism"—is to be found in P. Mussen and N. Eisenberg-Berg, *Roots of Caring, Sharing, and Helping* (W. H. Freeman, 1977).

5

Cultivating Tendencies by Discipline

At the basis of the moral life lie tendencies to act and refrain from acting in accord with moral law. If a girl is not disposed to keep her word in situations where she faces a choice between keeping and not keeping it, if a boy is not disposed to treat with equity persons of distinct races when in situations where he is confronted with racial diversity, and so on for all the other choices that face every one of us as human beings, then the very foundation of the moral life is missing. Surely discipline, with its two sides of reward and punishment, is one strategy by which tendencies to act and refrain from acting in certain ways—specifically, in accord with the moral law—can be cultivated in a person. The wisdom of the ages tells us this, and this wisdom is elaborately confirmed by contemporary psychological studies. Discipline, with its two sides of reward and punishment, is one way of altering a person's tendencies.

How do rewards and punishments work so as to alter a person's tendencies? Until recently, radical behaviorism was far and away the dominant current theory on this. Let us begin by looking briefly at what it says.

Radical behaviorism is a theory about how tendencies to act or behave in certain publicly observable ways are formed, suppressed, and altered. Most, if not all, behaviorists assume that almost all tendencies in human beings, normal and abnormal alike, are not indigenous to the organism but *learned*. What accounts for such learning is always the biological state of the organism plus publicly observable environmental stimuli.

In speaking of the biological state of the organism as a determinant of behavior, radical behaviorists wish to exclude all states of consciousness—such as beliefs, feelings, expectations—from their explanations. Some radical behaviorists hold that there are in fact no such things as states of consciousness; others disagree. But all contend that states of consciousness play no role whatever in explaining behavior. Indeed, those who hold that there are such entities as states of consciousness usually argue that the existence of these is a function of the biological state of the organism plus publicly observable environmental stimuli.

In any instance of human behavior, the radical behaviorist will look for five key factors. At the core will be some piece of observable behavior which is held to be the *response* to some antecedent events. These antecedent explanatory phenomena consist of some *observable stimulus*, plus the *biological state* of the organism. In turn, the response will have some *observable consequences* which are desirable, undesirable, or indifferent to the organism. Relating the response to the consequences which are relevant to the organism will be a certain *temporal schedule* (sometimes called a "contingency relationship"). For example, a child may experience the observable consequence of attention from its parents after a full minute of steady crying or after the first whimper.

With this picture in mind, how does the radical behaviorist theorize that rewards and punishments work to alter tendencies? They work as specimens of *operant conditioning*. Operant conditioning comes in two forms. The first involves a piece of behavior or a series of behaviors being followed at a certain interval by a consequence which is undesirable to the agent (*aversive*). The conditioning itself occurs when the behavior, as a result of that sequence being repeated on a certain schedule, is diminished or even extinguished. Extinguishing a two-year-old daughter's tendency to run out into the street by spanking her immediately when she does run out would be cited by the radical behaviorist as an instance of such operant conditioning. In the other form of operant conditioning a piece of behavior or a series of behaviors is followed at a certain interval by a consequence desirable to the agent; in this case the conditioning occurs when, as the result of repeating that sequence on a certain schedule, the behavior is reinforced—that is, the tendency to engage in that behavior is induced or strengthened. Reinforcing a schoolboy's behavior by giving him a piece of candy whenever he answers ten math problems correctly would be cited by the radical behaviorist as an instance of operant conditioning of this latter sort.

In the former instance, the consequence of the behavior functions as punishment; in this latter instance, as reward. But in both cases the consequences of the behavior alter the strength of the person's tendency to engage in it and even induce new tendencies. By a process known as feedback, the consequence of earlier behavior serves as stimulus to later behavior.

It has become clear in recent years that this very simple and elegant theory of how rewards and punishments work to alter our tendencies is in fact false. For one thing, rewards and punishments do not work only by way of operant conditioning. Furthermore, the radical behaviorist theory of how operant conditioning works is false. As the social learning theorist Albert Bandura remarked in a presidential address to the American Psychological Association, "contrary to popular belief, the fabled reflexive conditioning in humans is largely a myth."[1] Let us consider these two points in turn.

1. Behavior is sometimes altered not as the result of conditioning but as the result of observing what consequences happen to others because of their actions, or of being told what is likely to be the consequence of this or that action, or of reflecting on the likely consequences.[2] Suppose, for example, that I observe a driver speed down an icy highway and also see him spin out of control on a curve and crash into an oncoming car. On the basis of that observation my own tendencies while driving on icy roads may well be altered, even though I have never driven recklessly and thus never experienced the aversive consequence of doing so. Again, I may be *told* the consequences of operating a piece of heavy machinery after taking a certain medication. Because I believe that, my tendencies may be altered. Once again, I may not have experienced the consequences by performing the action in question. Finally there is the alteration of our tendencies which happens when we reflect on the consequences of what we

[1] Albert Bandura, "Behavior Theory and the Models of Man," *American Psychologist*, Dec. 1974.
[2] *Ibid.;* see also A. Bandura, "The Self System in Reciprocal Determinism," *American Psychologist*, Apr. 1978; and especially his book *Social Learning Theory* (Prentice-Hall, 1977).

might do. As Bandura puts it, "The extraordinary capacity of humans to use symbols enables them to engage in reflective thought, to create, and to plan foresightful courses of action in thought rather than having to perform possible options and suffer the consequences of thoughtless action."[3]

There is no plausible way of viewing these three ways of learning as versions of operant conditioning. In each type the tendency to act in certain ways is strengthened or weakened without the agent ever performing those actions. Instead, what happens in cases of observation, instruction, and reflection is that the person acquires certain *expectations* about what accompanies or follows from the action in question, and it is these expectations which are decisive in altering tendencies. Indeed, many recent studies conclude that actual consequences are less determinative of behavior than expected consequences. And though we may acquire such expectations by way of operant conditioning—that is, by performing the actions and suffering or enjoying the consequences—we may also acquire them by way of observation of others, by way of instruction, and by way of reflection and discovery. Human existence would be sorry indeed if this were not so.

2. Where operant conditioning does take place, the radical behaviorist thesis that this is always an automatic, noncognitive process is woefully false. Numerous laboratory experiments and field observations show that if we appeal to cognitions and affects (feelings) we can explain why human beings respond differently to the same stimuli, whereas without appealing to such states of consciousness no such explanation is available to us. As Bandura summarizes it,

> Originally, conditioning was assumed to occur automatically. On closer examination it turned out to be cognitively mediated. People do not learn despite repetitive paired experiences unless they recognize that events are correlated. . . . So-called conditioned reactions are largely self-activated on the basis of learned expectations rather than automatically evoked. The critical factor,

[3]Bandura, "The Self System in Reciprocal Determinism," *loc. cit.*, p. 345.

therefore, is not that events occur together in time, but that people learn to predict them and to summon up appropriate anticipatory reactions.[4]

If people are told the schedule of reinforcement pertaining to some action of theirs, they will not behave in the same way they would if left to discover the schedule on their own. And if they *never* become conscious of the schedule, they will behave quite differently yet.

We may summarize these points by saying that *actually* experienced rewards and punishments normally work in the same way as *anticipated* rewards and punishments, namely, by way of *expectations*. If you expect aversive consequences from a certain one of your actions, this will—others things being equal—diminish your tendency to perform that action. Similarly, if you expect desirable consequences to your actions, this will serve—other things being equal—to reinforce your tendency to perform those actions.

The fact that *expected* consequences are more determinative of behavior than *actual* consequences has important implications for parents and teachers. The most efficient way of inducing in students expectations about the consequences of their actions will normally also be the most efficient way of exerting a formative influence on their tendencies. And normally *telling* them what will happen if they act in a certain way is more efficient than saying nothing and allowing them to act and gradually to discover for themselves the desirable or aversive consequences paired off with their actions. The relevant advice then is this: State clearly to the child what consequences—rewards and punishments—are to be meted out for which actions. And then act consistently with this statement, lest the expectation be weakened or even destroyed.

[4]Bandura, "Behavior Theory and the Models of Man," *loc. cit.*, p. 859. For Bandura such *internal* consequences as feelings of guilt and self-satisfaction—along with expectations of these—have an important explanatory role. This addition of internal to the external consequences of our action marks another of Bandura's departures from radical behaviorism. He, along with social learning theorists in general, does remain a behaviorist in the *broad* sense of holding that all learning is determined either by classical conditioning, or by the actual and expected, internal and external, consequences of behavior.

In using rewards and punishments to shape tendencies, one must bear in mind that anticipated experiences are reinforcing or diminishing in their effects only relative to a person, a type of action, and a time. They are not inherently either diminishing or reinforcing in their effects. An anticipated experience which functions as reinforcement *for one person* may have no effect whatever on another. The promise that a child will be allowed to play baseball for an hour will have a highly motivating effect on one student, none on another. An anticipated experience which functions as reinforcement or diminishment for a given person *for one kind of activity* may not so function for another activity. Some things a person will do for pay, some other things not. And an anticipated experience which functions as reinforcement or diminishment for a given person for a certain kind of activity *at one time* may not so function at another time. In midmorning, the promise of a bed to sleep on in an hour will seldom encourage activity on a person's part, whereas late at night it will.

In reflecting on the use of rewards and punishments to shape tendencies, one should keep in mind the difference between *physical* punishments and rewards and *social* ones. The earliest punishments and rewards meted out to children by their fellow human beings are predominantly physical—spanking and the withdrawal of attractive objects are typical punishments, attractive food, toys, enjoyable activities are typical rewards. While physical rewards and punishments never cease—we remain, after all, physical creatures—social reinforcers and diminishers begin to play a greater and greater role: social approval or disapproval, praise or blame, the expression of love or the withdrawal of love become powerful reinforcers and diminishers (obviously more powerful for some persons than for others).

Thus far I have lumped rewards and punishments together. Many psychologists, however, contend that rewards are to be preferred to punishments. Many of the radical behaviorists, especially B. F. Skinner, claim that punishment is *less effective* a determiner of human action than rewards. Skinner argues that a person will characteristically seek to avoid the entire situation in which he or she expects punishment, rather than remaining in the situation and allowing his or her behavior to be altered. But of course one cannot always evade the situation; nor does all punishment consist of handing out something distasteful. Many punishments involve the removal of something desirable. "No gym for you today if you don't finish your math." As to whether punishment is in general less effective than rewards, we do not know; and, given the enormous diversity of punishments and rewards, we may never know. There is evidence, though, that in some situations the expression of *approval* is more effective than the expression of *disapproval;* and I know of no evidence of situations in which the opposite is true.

Certain kinds of punishment are obviously cruel and inhumane. Unfortunately, schools have traditionally provided many examples of just such punishment. But it can scarcely be contended that all forms of punishment are inhumane. Is it inhumane to express one's disapproval of someone's action? Conversely, it is obvious that certain forms of reward are, if not exactly inhumane, at least immoral. Knowing what we do about the effects of sugar on our bodies, it is probably immoral regularly to get children to do their schoolwork by holding out before them the promise of candy.

A third reason some have downgraded punishment is that it tends to stir up side-effects which outweigh whatever good there may be in the behavior it evokes. Depending on how severe it is, how inequitably it is distributed, how arbitrary its schedule, how acceptable or unacceptable the reasons given for administering or threatening it, punishment may evoke deep resentment.

But a full picture of the relative merits of punishments and rewards would also have to take account of the *desirable* side-effects of punishments. There is evidence, for example, that punishment plays a crucial role in the internalization of standards. (We shall return to this point in Chapter 8.) Then, too, it must not be supposed that rewards never have undesirable side-effects. Some fascinating experiments have shown that giving people extrinsic rewards for things they are intrinsically motivated to do may diminish their intrinsic motivation.[5]

---

[5]See especially Edward L. Deci, *Intrinsic Motivation* (Plenum Press, 1975); also Chapter 13 in L. Wheeler, *Interpersonal Influence* (Allyn & Bacon, second ed., 1978).

In one study, college students were presented an interesting puzzle to solve. Half the subjects were paid one dollar for each of four puzzles they solved, while the other half were given the same puzzles to solve but no pay. Later, all the subjects were left free in a situation where they could do a variety of other things, including solve more puzzles. The researchers found that the students who had not been offered payment for solving the puzzles were more inclined to continue working at them. A similar study found that children who were extrinsically rewarded for playing with a set of interesting magic markers and art materials were later less inclined to continue doing so than those who had not been so rewarded. College students threatened with an annoying buzzer if they did not solve some interesting puzzles within a certain time were less inclined to work on such puzzles later than those not so threatened. Praise for accomplishing some interesting task proved to have more ambiguous results, tending to decrease the intrinsic motivation of girls while heightening that of boys. Apparently the key factor here was the students' perception of the purpose of the praise. If they saw it as designed to control or manipulate them, their intrinsic motivation was diminished, whereas if they perceived it as designed to inform them how well they were doing, their sense of inner satisfaction was heightened.

As a result of the dominance, until recently, of radical behaviorism on the psychological scene, a certain *type* of reward/punishment strategy—the so-called behavior modification type—has gained a great many devotees in the schools. We shall conclude this discussion on discipline with a brief look at this strategy. In effect, behavior modification is simply the theory of radical behaviorism put to practical, technological use.

In order to understand behavior modification strategies, we must add one element to the description of radical behaviorism we gave earlier. The radical behaviorist holds that all learned behavior is learned either by way of *operant* conditioning (described above) or *classical* conditioning. Classical conditioning was first explored in detail early in this century by the Russian scientist Ivan Pavlov (1849–1936). It occurs when a stimulus S, which elicits a response R, and some environmental factor F, which does not elicit R, are conjoined in such a way that, at a later time, *F does* elicit *R*. A well-known example of this is Pavlov's discovery that he could make the ringing of a tuning fork elicit salivation in dogs if he conjoined the presentation of food sufficiently often and regularly with the ringing of the fork in the dog's presence. Another case of classical conditioning takes place when the occurrence of a *set* of stimuli, $S_1 \ldots S_n$, is scheduled in such a way that it elicits response *R* where previously *R* had not been elicited. For example, Pavlov discovered that he could induce "neurotic" behavior in dogs where no such behavior had been present before by altering the sequence of certain stimuli in various ways.

With this theory in mind the radical behaviorist makes recommendations concerning the modification of behavior. Notice in the first place that the goal is always the modification of *publicly observable behavior*. The radical behaviorist does not aim at removing unconscious conflicts, or stimulating insight, or altering personality traits. A second element in this strategy is to discover features of the *publicly observable environment* which can be manipulated to cause alterations in the behavior, in the manner of either classical conditioning or operant conditioning or some combination of the two. The radical behaviorist does not believe that cognitive factors have any effect on behavior. *Expectations* of consequences have nothing to do with determining behavior; behavior is determined by *actual* consequences ensuing upon *actually* performed actions. The radical behaviorist holds, indeed, that alterations in the biological state of the organism will also produce alterations in behavior but characteristically devotes little attention to this. Accordingly, surveying some situation with the five key factors in mind—*response, stimulus, biological state, consequences, temporal schedule*—the radical behaviorist interested in behavior modification will first try to pinpoint as accurately as possible the desired behavior. Then to change the behavior he or she will try either to alter the consequences of the behavior, or to alter the temporal schedule on which those consequences are offered, or to establish a regular conjunction between the stimulus and some factor in the environment which previously had nothing to do with this particular behavior.

A number of examples of such behavior modification may be found in a helpful survey by Wesley C. Becker entitled

"Application of Behavior Principles in Typical Classrooms."[6] The stimulus events in the experiment we shall look at were the behaviors of other persons—thus *social* reinforcers. The experiment reported studies of the combined effect of issuing rules, ignoring behavior which violates the rules, and praising behavior which conforms.

The researchers selected ten "problem children" from five elementary classrooms. Having defined a number of categories of behavior which disrupted learning or violated the rules (getting out of their seats, talking, making noises with objects, and the like), they trained observers to rate how often this type of behavior occurred during three twenty-minute sessions a week. The teachers were also observed to determine that the experiment was being carried out successfully.

After a five-week base line, the teachers began the experimental program, which had three components. The teacher's *rules* for classroom behavior were made explicit and repeated frequently. Teachers were also to *show approval* for appropriate behaviors (conducive to learning) and to ignore disruptive behaviors. If a child was hurting someone, the teacher could intervene as she saw fit. This rarely happened. The teachers were instructed to give praise for achievement, prosocial behavior, and following the rules of the group. They were to praise students for such behaviors as concentrating on individual work, raising hand when appropriate, responding to questions, paying attention to directions, following directions, sitting at desk, studying, and sitting quietly. They were instructed to use variety and expression in their comments and to smile when delivering praise. Teachers were to walk around the room during study time and give a pat on the back to children doing a good job. The teachers were given daily feedback regarding their effectiveness in showing approval contingent on appropriate behavior and in ignoring inappropriate behavior.

[6]In Carl E. Thoresen (ed.), *Behavior Modification in Education* (Univ. of Chicago Press, 1973). The primary report of Becker's experiment is found in an essay in *Journal of Special Education* (1967), I, 287–307.

The percentage of intervals of deviant behavior for the ten children dropped from 62.1 percent of the time during base line to 29.2 percent of the time during the experimental program when approval, ignoring deviant behavior, and rules were introduced.

In a later study it was found that issuing rules was not effective by itself. Reinforcement, consisting of praising the student when the rules were followed and ignoring the student when they were disobeyed, was necessary to make issuing rules effective.

In addition to social reinforcers, there are other reinforcers available to the classroom teacher. *Activity* reinforcers involve a pair of activities, one of which the children prefer to the other, arranged so that they are allowed to perform the preferred one only if they first perform the nonpreferred. With *object* reinforcers, children are given something desirable (such as a piece of candy) after performing the desired behavior. And of course punishment is also available, consisting either in taking away something the children desire or introducing something they dislike.

A version of object reinforcers which has caught the fancy of educators in recent years is so-called *token reinforcers*. This strategy rewards children with tokens of one sort or another, which they may later exchange for a wide variety of different objects or activities of their own choice. Tokens are conditioned reinforcers; in themselves they have no desirability. But their use enables the behavior-modifier both to make a variety of primary reinforcers available to the students, and to dispense those primary reinforcements over a period of time. This makes for much more flexibility in conditioning students who have different preferences and who are in different biological states. One devotee of behavior modification offers this vision of the school of the future, in which token reinforcers play a key role:

> It is suggested that whole schools be designed on the basis of reinforcement principles and of the concept of the token-reinforcer system. The fact is that a public school has very strong resources for reinforcement of all students, including those who are now considered to be learning problems because of retardation, emotional or behavioral disturbances, cultural deprivation, and so on.

Schools have special equipment for physical exercise, sports, games, dancing, painting, and the like. Most children do not have access to these sources of reinforcement at home and the activities that can occur in such facilities are very powerful reinforcers for them. In addition, schools offer some facilities for films and television, which could be expanded along with other reinforcing activities such as reading, special-interest clubs, and socializing. . . .

To repeat, it is proposed that we develop a whole school which is designed on positive reinforcement principles. The idea would be to provide reinforcing activities in the school which would maintain the child's coming to school. Within the school, the child would first report to a work-learning situation where he would perform work to a criterion, for which he would receive tokens.

After earning a certain number of tokens for work completed children would then be able to go on to a reinforcement period of their choice. This would be followed by another work-learning period, and so forth. . . . With systematic development and engineering and without the handicap of prejudice there would easily be an abundant source of reinforcement to maintain the effective learning of all children.[7]

Behavior-modification strategies, we said earlier, are a special version of reward/punishment strategies—a version faithfully in accord with radical behaviorist theory. Let me conclude with some critical remarks about using these particular versions of the reward/punishment strategy.

1. The limitation in such strategies to consequences *actually ensuing* upon actions *actually performed* is unwarranted. What counts in the determination of human action is not so much the *actual* consequences of actions *actually* performed as the *expected* consequences of actions that one *contemplates* performing. Such expectations may be built up by conditioning. But they may also be built up—usually more efficiently—by informing students of

[7]A. W. Staats, "Behavior Analysis and Token Reinforcement in Educational Behavior Modification and Curriculum Research," in *Behavior Modification in Education*, pp. 220–23.

what will follow from certain actions, or by allowing students to observe the consequences to others of acting that way. Behavior modification strategies are at best *one* way whereby the teacher can build up expectations in students as to the consequences of their actions, thus to have a formative influence on their tendencies.

2. Upon reading the description offered a few pages back of behavior modification strategy, all but the most deeply indoctrinated will have been struck by its manipulative character. This comes out at two points. For one thing, the teacher manipulates herself. She is instructed to smile and to utter words of praise. Now the proper function of uttering words of praise is to express praise, and the function of smiling at someone while uttering words of praise is surely to express one's approval and pleasure. The radical behaviorist overlooks this entirely and treats the words and the smile solely as reinforcers whose effect is to get someone else to act in a certain way. Thus dissembling and insincerity are built into the situation. The function of language and expression is debased. It is easy to see that if we in fact uttered declarative sentences solely because we wanted to influence people, not because we thought that the proposition expressed was true, and if we uttered words of praise solely because we wanted to influence people, not because we wanted to praise them, then shortly all genuine communication would be destroyed. We would be like the citizens of a totalitarian state who do not know whether they can or cannot trust what is officially said to them.

Perhaps worse, behavior modification strategies manipulate students. A deliberate attempt is made to short-circuit their nature as free, reflective, responsible creatures, aware of their environment, able to adopt standards for themselves, and capable of acting *on* those standards and in the light of that knowledge. Their potential as self-directing creatures, capable of acquiring a cognitive structure for morality *on which* they act, is ignored. They are treated entirely in terms of their resemblance to animals. Their dignity is ignored and violated.

Although rewards and punishments do indeed play a role in its formation, they do not by themselves *yield* the moral life.

The tendency to avoid acting in a racist manner may first be developed in children by rewards and punishments, but they are not yet moral agents until they act in nonracist fashion even when discipline is not in view, and do so by acting *on the principle* of love and respect.

The manipulative character of the behavior modification strategy comes out with special clarity in that grotesque vision of the school of the future. Part of what is appalling about that vision is that the rewards and punishments used are exclusively of the behavior modification sort. But more fundamentally, what appalls one is that here is a school which depends exclusively on discipline—no matter what sort. Missing is any concern to develop self-direction on the part of the students. Their actions are wholly determined by external consequences, which the teachers and administrators have introduced in order to get them, the children, to do what they, the adults, wish. Lacking, too, is any guarantee of carryover. Within the classroom and on the playground the students have been lured into doing what the teachers and administrators want them to do. But what happens when the students leave for home or move to another school? As Michael Scriven points out, "If one is mostly interested in behavior and its external conditions, one runs the risk of not focussing on the inner man. But only the inner man goes home after school, with the student. Only the inner man goes up to the next grade; the reinforcers do not."[8] And the reinforcers may in fact have acted destructively on the child's intrinsic motivation.[9]

Behaviorists have neglected these connected issues of self-directedness and transfer. Their entire interest has been to discover techniques for altering behavior by altering the environment. But with the breaking of the behaviorists' grip on experimental learning theory, a good deal of study has been devoted in recent years to the internalization of patterns of action and to the adoption of cognitive structures for morality. Later we

---

[8]Michael Scriven, "The Philosophy of Behavior Modification," in *Behavior Modification in Education*, p. 438.

[9]Deci, *op. cit.*, discusses some of the pro's and con's of using token economies in the schools.

shall be looking at some of these studies. Here let it simply be said that Skinner's apothegm, "A person does not act upon the world, the world acts upon him," is woefully false in its onesidedness.

By stressing the manipulative character of a school whose strategy of reward and punishment is exclusively that of behavior modification, and more generally, of a school which depends exclusively on discipline and ignores the need to cultivate in the student a cognitive structure for morality which is *internalized*, I do not mean to say that the use of pure behavior modification strategies is always an irresponsible affront to the dignity of the person. When such strategies are practiced on tiny children in whom the capacity for rational reflection and responsible choice has scarcely begun to develop, or on deeply disturbed adults in whom those capacities have been grievously wounded, or on rational adults who voluntarily submit to such strategies in order to overcome addictions, habits, mannerisms, and the like, the ethical issues on which we have focused in the preceding pages do not arise.

6

Cultivating Tendencies by Modeling

Our topic is still the fundamental dimension of the moral life: the tendency to act and refrain from acting in accord with the moral law. We have seen that discipline, with its two sides of reward and punishment, is one strategy for inculcating a tendency. We shall now look at another, known as modeling.

The wisdom of the ages tells us that children are influenced in what they tend to do by observing what those around them do—especially those for whom they feel admiration or affection. Likewise children are influenced by *representations* of what others do, in literature and drama, for example. It was on this ground that Plato proposed eliminating from his ideal republic all literature and drama which represented gods or humans doing what they should not be doing. During the last fifteen to twenty years, a large body of psychological experiments and studies has confirmed the wisdom of the ages on these matters.

The word "modeling" is typically used by psychologists to cover two related but somewhat different phenomena involving a subject observing someone performing some action. In one kind of modeling, the agent, as the result of such observation, acquires the *ability* to imitate the model. In the kind of modeling we shall focus on in this chapter, the agent, as the result of such observation, acquires the *tendency* to imitate the model—or the tendency to act thus is strengthened.

Modeling is indispensable for passing on to others many of the abilities we have acquired. Bandura's remarks are to the point:

> Because mistakes can produce costly, or even fatal consequences, the prospects for survival would be slim indeed if one could learn only by suffering the consequences of trial and error. For this reason, one does not

teach children to swim, adolescents to drive automobiles, and novice medical students to perform surgery by having them discover the appropriate behavior through the consequences of their successes and failures.... Apart from the question of survival, it is difficult to imagine a social transmission process in which the language, lifestyles, and institutional practices of a culture are taught to each new member by selective reinforcement of fortuitous behaviors, without the benefit of models who exemplify the cultural patterns.... If children had no opportunity to hear the utterances of models, it would be virtually impossible to teach them the linguistic skills that constitute a language.[1]

Perhaps the best way to grasp the significance of modeling as a strategy for cultivating tendencies is to look at the highlights of some of the experiments on modeling. A good place to begin is with those which explore the effects of modeling on resistance to temptation.

A 1967 study by A. H. Stein tested whether children confronted by temptation would imitate a model who yielded to or resisted the temptation.

The subjects were fourth-grade boys and the model was an adult male. The experimental temptation consisted of assigning the child to do a boring job while a highly attractive movie was shown just outside his line of vision. The job consisted of watching for a light and pushing a button when the light went on. The prohibition against looking at the movie was established by the experimenter's saying, "The lights probably won't come on very often so you may do whatever you like as long as you stay in your chair. You must stay in your chair, though, so you'll be ready when the lights do come on." The child was scored as yielding to temptation if he left his job to look at the movie.[2]

[1] *Social Learning Theory*, p. 12.
[2] Martin L. Hoffman, "Moral Development," in P. H. Mussen (ed.), *Carmichael's Manual of Child Psychology*, 3rd ed., II (John Wiley & Sons, 1970), 308. Stein's primary report is in *Child Development*, 38 (1967), 157–69.

Before being placed in the temptation situation, each child was put in one of three circumstances: (1) some children were presented with a model who resisted temptation; (2) some were presented with a model who yielded to temptation; (3) some were presented with *no* model. In each of the first two cases, the model indicated an interest in the movie by various motions and by commenting, "I sure wish I could see the movie."

What did Stein discover? Left alone in the room by the experimenter, the children who had observed the yielding model gave in to temptation more than those who had observed the resisting model, and also more than those who had observed no model. Those who had observed no model in fact yielded slightly less often than those who had observed the resisting model. Apparently modeling may *weaken* one's resistance to temptation, but it is not effective in *building up* resistance.

This conclusion is confirmed by other studies of how a model affects the way a subject responds to the prohibition of behavior which is ordinarily permitted, with this addition: among subjects who observe a yielding model being *punished* for yielding, resistance to temptation is not appreciably weakened. Also, observing a yielding model who is neither punished nor rewarded has the same effect on weakening resistance as observing a yielding model being rewarded. In short, a yielding model who is neither rewarded nor punished and a yielding model who is rewarded are equally effective in weakening resistance to temptation; whereas a yielding model who is punished and a nonyielding model are about the same in their effects as no model at all. (Actually, the punished yielding model and the nonyielding model both have a *slight* tendency to *weaken* resistance.)

Similar conclusions emerge from studies of the effect of models on behavior not ordinarily permitted. Studies of aggression show that those who observe an aggressive model punished are less likely to act aggressively than those who observe an aggressive model rewarded (and will act about the same as those not presented with a model at all). But once again, those who observe an aggressive model without observing that person either punished or rewarded act the same as do those who observe the model rewarded. It makes no difference whether the models are presented live or on film.[3]

A third type of situation is one in which a model adopts and lives up to a certain performance standard. A 1964 study by Albert Bandura and C. J. Kupers provides an example:

> Children participated in a bowling game with an adult or peer model. The scores, which could range from 5 to 30, were controlled by the experimenter. At the outset of the game the children and their models were given access to a plentiful supply of candy from which they could help themselves as they wished. Under one experimental condition, the model set a high standard for self-reward—on trials in which he obtained or exceeded a score of 20 he rewarded himself with one or two candies and made such self-approving statements as "I deserve some M & M's for that high score" or "That's great! That certainly is worth an M & M treat." In contrast, on trials in which he failed to meet the adopted standard he took no candy and remarked self-critically, "No M & M's for that" or "That does not deserve an M & M treat." In the other experimental condition the model exhibited a similar pattern of self-reward and self-disapproval except that he adopted the standard of 10, a relatively low level of performance. After exposure to their respective models, the children played the bowling game several times in succession. This was done in the absence of the model, although the experimenter and a research assistant were present. During these trials the children received a wide range of scores, and the performances for which they rewarded themselves with candy and self-approval were recorded.

The findings were as follows:

> The children's patterns of self-reward closely matched those of the model to which they had been exposed; moreover they tended to reproduce the self-approving and self-critical comments of their model. Thus, although both groups had access to a plentiful supply of candy, the children who had observed the model apply a

[3]*Ibid.*, pp. 312f.

high criterion of self-reward helped themselves to the candy sparingly and only when they achieved relatively high levels of performance, whereas children who were exposed to the low-standard model rewarded themselves generously even for minimal performance. A control group of children who were not exposed to models appeared to reward themselves randomly and for minimal performance.[4]

It is clear from this study and a number of others like it that an adult model's standards and patterns of self-reward significantly influence those of a child.[5] The evidence seems to be that not only do a model's low standards influence the student to lower the standards which otherwise he or she would adopt, but also a model's *high* standards influence the child to *raise* his or hers. However, the self-denial induced by a stringent model gives way rather readily when the subject is confronted by another model with lower standards.[6]

Considerably fewer studies have been made of the effects of models on altruistic acts and acts of kindness. The following, done in 1967 by D. Rosenhan and G. M. White, may be cited as a sample.

Fourth- and fifth-grade subjects played a bowling game— in which the scores had been programmed in advance— first taking turns with an adult model and later with no one else present. When the subject or the model obtained high scores he was awarded 5-cent gift certificates from a local department store. Each time the model won gift certificates he donated half of them to charity. The first time he won he said (ostensibly talking to himself), "I won. I believe I will give one certificate to the orphans each

---

[4]*Ibid.*, p. 313. The primary report is in *Journal of Abnormal Psychology*, 69 (1964), 1–9.

[5]Cf. Bandura, *Social Learning Theory*, p. 42.

[6]Hoffman's own conclusion is that "there is far more evidence that the observation of models is capable of undermining the effects of the child's past socialization in impulse control and self-denial than that it is an effective means of furthering these aspects of moral development. In brief, it appears that models can more readily reduce than increase the child's inhibition of impulse expression. There is also evidence that inhibitions resulting from modeling influences are highly vulnerable to counterinfluences such as the presence of self-indulging models" (*op. cit.*, p. 316).

time I win." On subsequent winnings he said nothing when making donations. The findings were that almost half the subjects who observed the model contributed in his absence, whereas none of the control subjects who saw no model did so. The occurrence of a prior positive or negative relationship with the model had no effect on the child's altruistic behavior.[7]

Though there are deficiencies in this study and others like it, it does seem that models who act kindly and altruistically thereby influence observers to act likewise.

Obviously a great many additional types of modeling situations can be analyzed. For our purposes it will be sufficient to look at just one other. In the studies cited thus far, the model either said nothing or said something which supported his actions in one way or another. But what we often confront in real life are situations in which a person preaches one thing while practicing another. What is the effect of such behavior?

J. H. Bryan and N. H. Walbeck reported in 1970 on a series of experiments, similar to the Rosenhan and White experiment just mentioned, concerning the effects of such inconsistency on third- and fourth-graders.[8] A typical experiment was one in which model and subject played a bowling game, for which they received redeemable certificates as prizes. On the table was a box with the words "donations for the poor children." Various combinations were devised of models practicing either generosity or selfishness, while at the same time preaching generosity, or preaching selfishness, or preaching something neutral, or not preaching at all. The "generous" model would put one of every three certificates won into the donation box; the "selfish" model put none into the box. A model preaching generosity would say things like "If I win any money today, I am going to give some to those poor children. She said we didn't have to, but I think it would be a good idea—it would make them happy." A model who preached selfishness would say "If I win any money today, I am not going to give any to the poor children" or "No, sir, why

[7]*Ibid.*, p. 324. The primary report is in *Journal of Personal Social Psychology*, 4 (1967), 424–31.

[8]J. H. Bryan & N. H. Walbeck, "Preaching and Practicing Generosity: Children's Actions and Reaction," *Child Development*, 41 (1970), 329–53.

should we give any of our money to other people?" Or a model might simply make neutral preachments.

Sometimes the model preached what he practiced, sometimes his preaching was inconsistent with his practice, sometimes he simply preached without practicing, sometimes he practiced without preaching. In one experiment the model was an adult; in another, a child. This seemed to make no difference. In some of the experiments a film of the model was shown; in others, the model was presented live. That, too, seemed to make no difference.

The decisive determinant of how the children would act was always the *action* of the model. The children tended to practice as the model practiced and *preach as the model preached!* The practice of generosity on the part of the model increased generous behavior in the child. Likewise the *preaching* of generosity on the part of the model increased the behavior of *preaching* generosity in the child. But the preaching of generosity by itself did not increase the practice of generosity; and the preaching of generosity while practicing greed weakened the effects of the practice of greed only slightly.[9] In general, it made very little difference what the model preached. Overwhelmingly it was the model's practice that influenced the practice of the subject, with the preachment having just a slight tendency to diminish the effects of practice if the two were inconsistent. Preaching induced *preaching* rather than practice.

In all the experiments cited, the subject had no choice as to who would be the model in the situation studied nor was it ever ambiguous which of all the model's actions was to function as the action modeled. But in real life we always have many options as to whom and what to model ourselves on. Nobody can imitate everybody on everything. Nobody can even imitate *anybody* on everything. What determines *which* kinds of persons are most susceptible to modeling influence by *which* kinds of people for *which* kinds of actions?

---

[9]There is some evidence that elaborated exhortation which is quite specifically focused on the situation does have an effect, even approaching that of practice after a sizable lapse of time. See Grusec, Saas-Kortsaak, and Simutis, "The Role of Example and Moral Exhortation in the Training of Altruism," *Child Development,* 49 (1978), 920–23.

The studies which have tried to discover what sorts of persons are most susceptible to modeling influences tend to have design deficiencies, so that not much can be said about this. Similarly, there is little information on *which* features of a person's behavior are most likely to be imitated. But it is clear which sorts of persons a given person is most likely to imitate; namely, those high in his or her affection or esteem on account of their prestige, power, intelligence, competence, and the like.[10]

Though much remains unknown concerning the detailed workings of modeling, we do understand enough to realize that this is a critically important phenomenon for the conduct of education, whether by parents or teachers. A Christian philosophy of education, I have suggested, considers its proper goal to be equipping and training the child for responsible action. From the modeling experiments we learn that a key factor in attaining this goal is whether those persons whom the child takes as models are themselves living a life of responsible action. That is a sobering thing to learn—or rather to have confirmed.

Traditional teacher training concentrates on lesson plans, assignments, lectures, worksheets, and the like. Nothing to be learned from the modeling experiments shows that these are unimportant components of the educational process. Yet those experiments do force us to conclude, with respect to the shaping of student tendencies, that how teachers *comport* themselves is even more important than what they say. Teachers— certainly *good* ones—are almost inevitably impressive members of the child's world and thus prime candidates for decisive modeling influence. It is sheer fantasy to suppose that one can have a formative influence on the knowledge and abilities of the student and leave uninfluenced and unmodified his or her tendencies. Teachers or administrators who act mean-spiritedly will thereby increase the incidence of mean-spirited acts in their students. No amount of noble or pious words will cover that up.

There is another sobering thing to be learned from the experiments on modeling. We saw that although modeling can apparently induce children to adopt higher standards for them-

[10]See A. Bandura, *Psychological Modeling* (Aldine/Atherton, 1971), pp. 54ff.

selves than if left to their own devices, this effect is very fragile, and tends to work only so long as a counter-model does not appear on the scene. In general, experiments which have tested the effects of contradictory models show that such dissonance yields, statistically, about the same result as if no models at all had been presented. Some children will tend to imitate one of the models, some the other, some neither.

The Christian school is constantly confronted by contradictions between the kind of life that it—at its best—tries to model, and the kind of life that the child meets outside of school. Conflict may arise between the school and its supporting constituency. The school, perhaps, raises questions about America First-ism and its teachers try in their lives to shun this heresy, while its supporting constituents run God and nation together.[11] Even more fundamentally, the Christian school, if it acts as it ought, will constantly find itself out of step with the surrounding culture. Yet because its task is not to insulate the students from that culture but rather to prepare them to live and work in it, the situation is bound to arise in which the children are confronted with dissonant models. The modeling experiments force us to ask whether *alternative* education is really possible except under conditions of complete isolation.

What makes this question inescapable is that it makes no appreciable difference whether models are presented *live* or by way of representations on film or television. We noted this in connection with several experiments, but it is so important that we should perhaps cite one further experiment, chosen from a multitude of relevant ones. In a 1972 study by Leifer and Roberts 271 children (40 kindergarteners, 54 third-, 56 sixth-, 51 ninth-, and 70 twelfth-graders) viewed television programs which included various amounts of aggression.

These programs covered the range usually watched by children of these ages and were taken directly off the air and shown without editing. Immediately after viewing,

[11]Not that in every case of conflict the school is right and the constituents wrong! I have all too vividly in mind tales of loving parents confronted by harsh, repressive, arbitrary, authoritarian Christian schools.

the child was questioned about his understanding of the motivations and consequences for the violence in each program; then he was asked to choose among various behavioral options in hypothetical conflict situations that were presented in story and slide form. The amount of aggression in the program watched was one of the best predictors of how aggressive the child's behavioral choices were, while the context of what he had seen, defined in terms of motivations and consequences, did not relate to aggression at all and thus failed to serve as a "controlling cue."[12]

All other experiments came to the same conclusion: observing incidents of violence on film or television tends to increase the incidence of acts of violence among observers—and it makes no difference whether in the story situation the acts of violence were justified or not.

Is an alternative education which is Christian possible under nonisolation conditions? We would make two observations which contribute to answering this absolutely fundamental question. In the first place, the resistance of children to "outside" influence is very much strengthened if they are surrounded by a loving, supporting community. Masses of evidence in social psychology show that people strongly tend to adopt the beliefs and attitudes of a community in which they find love and acceptance. Experiencing such a community makes them more resistant to models in conflict with that community than they would otherwise be. Thus the success of Christian education in a secularized context depends a great deal on whether the students experience a loving, sustaining community in school, home, and church. When love is absent, the school will fail.

Second, some interesting research on the effects of psychological "inoculation" is relevant to the question we are considering. For example, researchers formulated a number of medical claims widely accepted as truisms—for example,

---

[12]R. M. Liebert and R. W. Poulos, in Thomas Lickona (ed.), *Moral Development and Behavior* (Holt, Rinehart & Winston, 1976), p. 291. This essay includes reports of several relevant experiments. The experiment described here is taken from the U.S. government study *Television and Social Behavior* (Government Printing Office, 1972), II, 43–180.

"Everyone should get an annual physical checkup, even if one is not bothered by any symptom of illness." A series of experiments was designed to determine what kind of defense best prepares a person to meet strong attacks on these truisms. For one group of subjects the researchers prepared a *reassuring* defense of the truisms, giving arguments in favor of them and citing no objections. Another group was given a *threatening* defense, which cited objections to the truisms and offered refutations of these objections. A third group received no defense.

Immediately after these two kinds of defenses were presented, the belief-level of those who received the reassuring defense was higher than that of those who received the threatening defense. But when these two groups were presented with a strong attack on the truism, and no refutation of the attack, then the belief-level of those who had been presented a threatening defense was significantly higher than that of those who had been presented with a reassuring defense—and it was considerably higher than the belief-level of the control group, which had received no prior defense. Surprisingly it made little difference whether or not the arguments used in the attack were the same as those presented and refuted in the threatening defense. The new-argument attack had only slightly more tendency to weaken the strength of belief in the threatening-defense group than the same-argument attack.[13]

The conclusion is obvious. The best defense against attacks on the consensus (truisms) of one's community is inoculation—presenting and then refuting arguments against the elements of that consensus. Inoculation is far more effective than no defense at all, or reassuring defenses which never so much as mention objections. As McGuire puts it: "A believer's faith in his culture's ideological truisms tends to have a spurious strength, analogous to the deceptive physical robustness of an animal brought up in a germ-free environment. Both are extremely vulnerable to attacking material and both gain resistance from preexposure to a weakened dose of the threatening material."[14]

[13]Wm. J. McGuire, "A Vaccine for Brainwash," in *Readings in Psychology Today*, 3rd ed. (CRM Books, 1974), pp. 344–48.
[14]*Ibid.*, p. 348.

What psychological mechanisms are at work in modeling? Why does observation of behavior, under certain circumstances, heighten the tendency to that behavior in the observer? We do not know. Perhaps there is in fact no one mechanism at work. A number of theories have been proposed (conveniently reviewed by Albert Bandura in the introduction to *Psychological Modeling*), but none has gained consensus. In any case, it seems unlikely that the only mechanism at work in modeling is that by observing the actions of others we acquire expectations concerning aversive and desirable consequences of our own actions. Instead, it looks as if there is in humanity a tendency to imitate those who are loved or esteemed.

7

Internalizing Tendencies

I suggested earlier that tendencies to act and to refrain from acting in accord with the moral law lie at the foundation of the moral life. In the preceding two chapters we saw how contemporary psychological studies confirm the wisdom of the ages that discipline and modeling are effective strategies for cultivating such tendencies. Now we move to the second dimension of the structure of the moral agent: the *internalization* of those tendencies. How can the internalization of a tendency to act in accord with the moral law be induced?

A tendency to act in a certain way is always a tendency to act thus *under certain circumstances*. Suppose that as the result of discipline, children acquire the tendency to tell the truth when they expect to be rewarded for so doing or punished for not so doing, but acquire no tendency to tell the truth when they believe that discipline is not in prospect. Obviously such children are not yet fully moral agents. The situations in which we ought to act in accord with the moral law do not coincide with situations in which we expect the external consequences of so acting to be pleasant or of not so acting to be aversive. If discipline works simply by inducing expectations of external rewards and punishments, something more is needed.

Let me describe this deficiency of punishment a bit more carefully. Suppose our goal is to cultivate in the child the tendency to tell the truth in a certain kind of circumstance—let us call it K—and (to make matters simple) that some ten examples of circumstance K come the child's way in the course of a lifetime. The strategy behind discipline is deliberately to attach rewards and/or punishments to a selection of these—perhaps the first five, (1) through (5)—and, more importantly, to induce in the child the *expectation* that rewards and punishments are attached to these. Perhaps the child actually performs (1) and (2), and, given the expectations this induces, goes on to tell the truth in (3) through (5) also.

But now what about (6) through (10), which may arise in the course of adult life? In the case of (8), let us say, praise may be expected for telling the truth and chastisement for lying. So the discipline experienced will be relevant there. But in the other cases there is no such expectation, and, indeed, in cases (6) and (7) one may expect some rather unpleasant consequences for telling the truth.

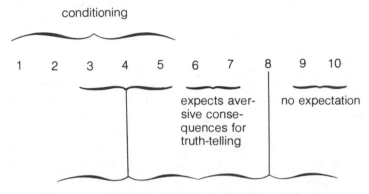

The conditioning experienced in (1) and (2) makes discipline an adequate strategy for getting the person to tell the truth in (3) through (5) and (8). But we want the person to tell the truth *in all these instances*, (1) through (10). And discipline comes up short, particularly for the problematic cases (6) and (7).[1] Worse, discipline may not only fail to produce a tendency to tell the truth in a good share of cases, but it may actually inculcate the tendency to tell the truth *when and only when* one expects the consequences of truth-telling to be pleasant or lying to be unpleasant. So discipline will not merely have left us looking for

[1]This actually overstates the case. What I say would be true only if discipline worked *solely* by inducing expectations concerning external rewards and punishments. But under some circumstances it seems also to produce guilt feelings upon departure from the pattern, and these guilt feelings seem to have a motivational effect. Thus punishment *is* relevant to internalization.

some other strategy to handle (6), (7), (9), and (10), but will have provoked a wrong tendency.

How are the shortcomings of discipline to be overcome? And how do we prevent it from inducing the immoral tendency, for example, to tell the truth when and only when one expects the consequences of so doing to be more pleasant than those of not so acting? It seems clear that modeling sometimes works in essentially the same way as discipline; namely, by inducing expectations concerning the external consequences of one's actions. In such cases, modeling will have the same shortcomings and deficiencies as discipline. It is not clear, however, that all cases of modeling work this way. But then the point to be made is that the tendencies induced purely by modeling are often rather fragile, susceptible to destruction by countermodels. That raises the question of how tendencies to act in accord with moral law can be made enduring in the face of countermodels?

Psychologists would express these questions in terms of *internalization.* How can tendencies to act in certain ways in certain circumstances be *internalized?* How can one cultivate in a person the tendency to act thus and so in this or that circumstance regardless of any expectation of desirable consequences? Until such internalization has taken place, a moral agent has not yet emerged. Martin L. Hoffman's essay "Moral Development" offers an elaborate overview of the contemporary literature on internalization, and a summary of his conclusions will provide a good sketch of what can be learned from contemporary studies.

Four distinct phenomena appear in the literature as criteria for judging how thoroughly a person has internalized some regularity of action: (1) the extent to which the person *resists pressure to deviate* from the regularity (this seems to me the core of the concept of internalization); (2) the degree to which the person *feels guilt upon deviating* from the regularity; (3) the degree to which the person *avoids appealing to external sanctions* when asked why he thinks the regularity should be followed; and (4) the extent of the person's tendency to *confess and accept responsibility for deviating* from the regularity.

From the literature on parental child-rearing Hoffman distills three fundamental techniques which investigators have probed for their effects on internalization. The first of these is *power assertion.* This includes physical punishment, deprivation of things or privileges, direct application of force, and the threat of any of these.

> In using these techniques the parent seeks to control the child by capitalizing on his physical power or control over material resources. Rather than rely on the child's inner resources (e.g., guilt, shame, dependency, love, or respect) or provide him with information necessary for the development of such resources, the parent punishes the child physically or materially, or relies on his fear of punishment.[2]

Power assertion, in other words, consists in using and threatening to use physical reinforcers and diminishers.

A second type of technique Hoffman calls *love-withdrawal* techniques:

> The parent simply gives direct but nonphysical expression to his anger or disapproval of the child for engaging in some undesirable behavior. Examples are ignoring the child, turning one's back on him, refusing to speak or listen to him, explicitly stating a dislike for the child, and isolating or threatening to leave him.[3]

Techniques of a third type Hoffman calls *induction* techniques. Here the parent or teacher gives *reasons* for the child to act in accord with some regularity of action.

> Examples are pointing out the physical requirements of the situation or the harmful consequences of the child's behavior for himself or others. . . . Also included are techniques which appeal to conformity-inducing agents that already exist, or potentially exist, within the child. Examples are appeals to the child's pride, strivings for mastery and to be 'grown up,' and concern for others.[4]

Hoffman singles out for special attention other-oriented reasons, in which the parent makes appeal to the implications of the child's behavior for other persons.

The conclusions are striking. No matter which criterion

---

[2]Hoffman, *loc. cit.*, p. 285.
[3]*Ibid.*
[4]*Ibid.*, p. 286.

for internalization is used to judge the results, power assertion does nothing whatever to promote the internalization of tendencies. Fairly often, in fact, it has a negative impact. The technique of love withdrawal also proves, on the whole, not to have any impact on internalization. The few cases in which it promoted internalization are counterbalanced by instances in which it had a negative impact.

> Love withdrawal does make the child more susceptible to adult influence but this has no necessary bearing on moral development. The one contribution to socialization that love withdrawal appears to make is to produce anxiety, which leads to the renunciation of hostile impulses and perhaps other impulses as well. These findings offer no basis for altering the conclusion ... that love withdrawal alone is an insufficient basis for the development of those capacities—such as guilt and internal moral judgment—which are commonly thought of as critical characteristics of a fully developed, mature conscience.[5]

The best technique for promoting internalization is induction— the offering of reasons, particularly other-oriented reasons, that is, reasons pointing out to the child how the other person would feel. And induction is particularly effective when the reasons are offered by a parent accustomed to show affection to the child.

Unfortunately, this is a rather rough and crude conclusion. One wants to know *what sorts* of reasons are especially effective and why they work, but on these questions one gets little direct information. Indeed, in what Hoffman says about induction he lumps together a motley group of reasons, including those which point out "the physical requirements of the situation or the harmful consequence of the child's behavior for himself." Such reasons operate in essence no differently from discipline— at least once the child discovers the "schedule" on which the punishment occurs. For as we have observed several times, it is the *expectation* of aversive consequences, more than the aversive consequences themselves, that determines behavior. Yet it would be incorrect to conclude that in the effectiveness of reasons for inducing internalization we only have, under another

[5] *Ibid.*, p. 302.

guise, the workings of external rewards and punishments.

For one thing, as Hoffman remarks, it proves to be true that *other-oriented* reasons are the *most* effective ones. Again, we get no explanation for why this is so. Do such reasons tap an impulse of *empathy* in the child? Does the command to love our neighbor as ourselves echo a deep impulse in our psychological nature? No such questions are answered in Hoffman's review. But whatever the psychological workings, research shows that the offering of other-oriented reasons is an effective technique for securing internalization.

Also included within the grab-bag of reasons Hoffman groups under induction are those which appeal "to the child's pride, strivings for mastery and to be 'grown up.'" These are reasons which appeal to *internal* consequences of the child's action. And in noticing the relevance of internal consequences of our actions we enter a crucial domain entirely neglected by the radical behaviorists, who concentrate all their attention on the external consequences. It is perfectly obvious, however, that our actions also have internal consequences, in particular, *feelings* of various sorts: guilt, accomplishment, pride, shame, and the like. It seems obvious that such feelings are strong motivators to action; and that, when relevant, internalization can be induced by appealing to such reasons. In fact, there are those who argue (Albert Bandura, for example) that all internalization of tendencies is to be explained thus.

In the third place, if one looks now at experiments relevant to internalization, it becomes clear that even inscrutable reasons can be effective, at least for children. Let us look, for example, at a pair of experiments performed by Justin Aronfreed. I shall quote extensively from his summary.

The first of the experiments was conducted with boys and girls ranging from eight to ten years old. The results were the same for both sexes.

> The experiment begins with a training period in which the individual child is presented, over a series of ten successive trials, with different pairs of very small toy replicas of real and familiar common objects. Although the toys vary from one trial to another, one of the toys in each pair is always highly attractive, while the other is relatively unattractive and nondescript. In each trial the

child is asked to pick up the toy that he wants to tell about, to hold it briefly in his hand, and then to tell something about the toy when requested to do so. Somewhere within this sequence of behavioral components, the child is punished during any trial in which he chooses the attractive toy. The punishment consists of verbal disapproval ("*No!*") and deprivation of candy by the experimental agent of socialization, without any further explanation (other than that implied in the original instructions, which simply warn the child that some choices are not permitted, without specifying which ones).

The timing of the punishment with respect to the onset and termination of a transgression sequence varies in four steps, which represent distinct experimental training conditions. But the timing remains consistent over trials for the subjects within any one of these conditions. In contrast, the subject is always permitted to choose and tell about an unattractive toy without punishment. Although the children invariably begin with choices of the attractive toys, they learn very quickly in this type of training. Almost all of them begin to choose the unattractive toy after only one or two punishments. And they continue to do so throughout the trials.

The really interesting observation occurs during a common test for internalization, which directly follows all four of the different training conditions. The child is left alone on a carefully prepared pretext, under conditions which free him of any apparent risk of surveillance. Again he is confronted with a pair of small toys [one attractive and the other not]. . . . After the training condition in which punishment is introduced quite early in the sequential components of the act of transgression (while the child is still reaching), the majority of children never touch the attractive toy during the test for internalization. Other children in this condition succumb to temptation only after a long period of resistance. But for virtually all children who have been punished *during* training at the latest point in the act of transgression (after telling about the toy), handling of the attractive toy usually begins almost immediately when the experimental agent leaves the room. . . .

After the experimental session is over, the children are questioned about their choices of toys during both training and test. Almost none of them can verbalize anything that even approaches an evaluative standard. In trying to account for their actions, they refer uniformly only to the danger of external punishment (in the presence of the agent).[6]

One appropriate conclusion is that punishment does not work *solely* by inducing expectations in the person concerning the desirable and undesirable consequences of his or her actions. Rather, punishment *performed under certain conditions* itself has some internalizing effects. The children's *expectations* when the experimenter left the room were presumably the same; yet, depending on how they were punished, the tendency not to pick up the attractive toys was far more internalized in some than in others. A common account of why punishment administered under certain conditions has an internalizing effect is that it produces in the agent feelings of guilt, regret, or the like, upon departure from the induced pattern of action.

Without in any way playing down the significance of the apparent internalizing effect of punishment itself, when administered under certain conditions, I want to call attention to a second, comparative experiment performed by Aronfreed with *reasons* introduced. The method was the same, with only the following modifications.

> During the training trials of all of the new variations, punishment is delayed until six seconds after the child's completion of a transgression (choosing and picking up the attractive rather than the unattractive toy). This interval of delay of punishment was the third of the four timing variations used in the original experiment. . . . Now the experimental agent of socialization introduces, into the delayed-punishment condition, a verbalized cognitive structure which the child can use to represent certain properties of the transgression. During the initial instructions, and together with each occurrence of punishment, the agent states that certain toys are "*hard to tell about*" and are therefore "*only for older boys (girls)*." The agent's verbalization is preceded by the

[6]"Moral Development from the Standpoint of a General Psychological Theory," in Lickona, *op. cit.*, pp. 57f.

verbal disapproval ("*No!*") and coterminous with the deprivation of candy, so that it will be interwoven with components of punishment.

It will be observed that the agent injects a cognitive structure of ease versus difficulty into the child's choice of which toy to tell about. But this structure does not specify any particular category of toy. Nor is it especially rational or appropriate (and purposely so) for a distinction between attractive and unattractive toys. Nevertheless, the verbal provision of this structure during punishment training induces more effective suppression of handling of the attractive toy during the test for internalization. Children who are exposed to this form of training show more prolonged internalized suppression than was shown by children who were trained without cognitive structure (but under the same delay of punishment) in the original experiment. And most of the children who are given cognitive structure are able to verbalize the standard of ease versus difficulty, when they are asked after the experiment to explain their predominant choices of unattractive toys during training.[7]

What strikes one about the children's response to the reason the experimenter offered them is that, odd though it is, they accept it from him. They themselves offer it when questioned later. Furthermore, they evidently accept it in two different ways: (1) they believe that it *applies*, that the more attractive toys *are* more difficult to describe; and (2) it becomes a reason for them *on which* they themselves act as they do.

Aronfreed concludes that the increased internalization in such situations results from the experimenter's having offered the child an acceptable way of cognitively structuring the situation. Hoffman agrees: "The effectiveness of induction as discipline, as compared to power assertion and love withdrawal, appears to be based less on the fear of punishment and more on the child's connecting its cognitive substance with his own resources for comprehending the necessities in the situation and controlling his own behavior accordingly."[8]

It seems likely that reasons will in general be effective in securing internalization only if they are accepted—in the double

---

[7]*Ibid.*, pp. 60f.
[8]*Loc. cit.*, p. 286.

sense that they are believed to apply to the situation and that they are acted on. If so, one would of course expect some reasons to be more effective than others for internalizing a tendency. The more effective ones will be those which more obviously apply, and those on which the subject is more willing to act. This is borne out by another Aronfreed experiment, a variant on the one just cited:

> Another training variation injects the same cognitive structure of ease versus difficulty into the child's choice within each pair of toys. But it focuses the agent's explanation of punishment on the child's *intention*. Each time that a transgression occurs, the agent coordinates punishment with a statement that the child had "*wanted*" to pick up a toy that was "*hard to tell about*." This focus on intention produces a very effective suppression... which is fully comparable to that shown by children who were punished during training immediately upon reaching for an attractive toy (under the original condition of no provision of cognitive structure). A great many of these intention-trained children never handle the forbidden toy during the test for internalization. The remainder do so only quite late in the ten-minute test period.[9]

We ought not to exaggerate the decisiveness of these studies. But they do quite clearly lead to the conclusion that an effective strategy for inducing a child to internalize a tendency is to offer a *reason* for acting in accord with that particular regularity—for example, "because things hard to describe are to be avoided." To be effective, the reason must single out some property or properties which the child will believe to belong to the actions in question. They need not *in fact* belong to those actions. The attractive toys in the experiments we reviewed were probably no more difficult to describe. But the children must *believe* that they belong to the actions. Secondly, to be effective the reason offered must be a principle that the child will adopt as his or her own reason for acting in a certain way. It must be a standard which the child *internalizes*. In short, the best way to induce a child to internalize a tendency is to supplement one's

[9] *Loc. cit.*, p. 61.

discipline and modeling by citing as a reason for acting thus a principle (standard) which the child believes to apply to the actions in question and which he or she internalizes.

To parents and teachers who wish to internalize the child's tendencies to act in accord with moral law, we can say this: Give the child *reasons*. Do not just discipline him or her to act in accord with moral law. Do not only depend on inarticulate modeling. Give an acceptable reason for acting thus. But reasons alone will generally be ineffective in producing tendencies. Discipline and modeling, supported by reasons, are the most effective strategy known for inducing internalized tendencies to act in certain ways.

I have said almost nothing in this chapter about the "moral emotions." Yet it has often been argued that an agent's internalization of a pattern of action is inextricably connected with his or her feeling guilty or ashamed or regretful or disgusted when he or she has acted out of accord with that pattern. This seems correct. The internalization of a pattern of action does seem to be intimately linked with the arousal of negative emotions by one's violation of that pattern. Where these "moral emotions" are absent, internalization has not occurred. As Aronfreed says, "moral education must build upon the strong affective dispositions acquired in early experience . . . affective values are, as it were, the ultimate axiomatic base upon which moral principles can engage the child's conduct among and toward others."[10] The psychological mechanisms at work in us when we feel guilt or shame or regret upon violating a certain pattern of action, remain obscure. Nonetheless, whatever the mechanism, current research indicates that one way of attaching feelings of guilt to the violation of a certain pattern of action is for an affectionate person to combine discipline with reasons.[11] For our purposes here, that is the important thing.

[10] *Ibid.*, p. 64.

[11] According to Aronfreed, "a moderate amount of verbalization of standards to the child, particularly when it focuses on his intentions, will yield much more effective internalized control than might be expected if the control depended on the coincidence between overt action and punishment. And . . . there are very strong indications that the representations transmitted by verbalization must, in order to be effective, be given an affective value by a fairly precise association with punishment" (*ibid.*, p. 63).

8

Cognitive Structures for Morality

The moral life, I have said repeatedly, is based on tendencies to act in accord with moral law. One way to inculcate in persons the tendency to act in a certain way is to arouse in them the expectation that desirable external consequences will follow if they act thus and/or undesirable external consequences will follow if they do not. Among such desirable and undesirable consequences are rewards and punishments. *Discipline* can be used to inculcate tendencies.

But acting in accord with moral law often requires the agent to act or not to act in a certain way even without expectations of desirable or undesirable external consequences. Sometimes it even requires acting in the expectation of *undesirable* external consequences. Accordingly, parents and teachers must often aim at getting the child to internalize tendencies to act in accord with moral law.

How can this be done? How can we induce in someone a *general* tendency to tell the truth, regardless of whether the expected external consequences of truth-telling in a given case are desirable? From the evidence summarized in Chapter 7 the best way seems to be accompanying discipline and modeling with a *reason* for so acting. As we saw, not just any reason will do. One must offer a reason such that the agent believes that the principle cited in it applies to those actions and tends to perform these actions *for the reason that* the principle applies to them. In other words, the *standard* cited in the reason must be *internalized* by the agent, and he or she must believe that it fits those actions.[1] Not to pick up attractive toys because they are hard to describe is

---

[1]Notice that here I am speaking of *standards* as internalized. Up to this point I have spoken of *tendencies* as internalized. A standard is internalized in a person when he or she tends to act on it.

to have internalized the standard, "Picking up things which are hard to describe is to be avoided," and to believe that the standard applies to these toys.

But how does one induce someone to internalize a standard? Of course, our concern here is not with arbitrary standards like that of the experiment—"picking up things which are hard to describe is to be avoided"—or with practical hints like "planing the wood against the grain is to be avoided." Our concern here is with *moral* standards. How can we induce a child to internalize moral standards?

To be a fully moral agent one must always act *in accord with* moral law. But one need not always act *on* some moral standard which coincides with the law. That is, one's *reasons* for acting a certain way need not always be the acceptance of some moral standard: sometimes people act as they ought to act out of habit or impulse. Still, in a world of moral conflict and sinful tendencies, it seems evident that the moral agent will to a considerable extent have to *act on* moral principles. One must to a considerable extent *internalize* moral standards.

So we see psychological strategy and moral requirement coming together. The evidence of the experiments cited in the preceding chapter suggests what is the best way to induce people to internalize the tendency to act in accord with the moral law: namely, induce them to internalize a moral standard they themselves believe to fit those situations. Now we see that in this world people cannot even *be* moral agents unless they often *act on* moral standards. They cannot be moral agents unless they often have a reason for acting as they do, a reason which includes their acceptance of some moral standard. In this way the requirements for being a moral agent coincide with the best strategy for internalizing tendencies. If a person is to become a moral agent he or she must internalize moral standards. And the best way to induce a person to internalize the tendency to act in accord with the moral law is to induce that person to internalize the relevant moral standard. The recommendations of psychology and the requirements of morality interlock. So it is doubly important to ask how persons can be induced to internalize moral standards.

Consider an instance in which a moral standard is cited as a reason for not acting in a certain way. "Don't use the company postage meter for your personal letters," someone might say to a fellow employee at the office, "because that's really embezzling and embezzling is (morally) wrong." The moral standard appealed to here is "Embezzling is wrong." Now if our clerk is to internalize (tend to act on) that principle, he or she must, in the first place, have acquired the moral concept *wrong*. And in general, one cannot internalize any moral principle whatever until one has acquired the moral concepts—*right, wrong, ought,* and so forth. If one has not acquired these concepts, then one cannot grasp principles which use them, and one cannot act on a principle that one doesn't grasp.

Furthermore, in order to internalize some genuinely *moral* principle—that is, one which coincides with the moral law—one must be able (to this extent at least) to apply the moral concepts (*right, wrong, ought,* etc.) correctly. To internalize the principle that embezzling is wrong one must know that the concept *wrong* applies to cases of embezzling. If one somehow acquired the moral concepts but always applied them mistakenly—judging embezzling to be right, aiding the crippled to be wrong, etc.—then though one might internalize some principle in which the moral concepts *occur*, they would not be *moral* principles. That is to say, they would not be principles which coincide with the moral law.

To summarize, a person cannot internalize genuinely moral principles without *grasping* moral concepts and (to some extent) *knowing how* to apply those concepts correctly.

This same point can be put in a different way with the concept of a *cognitive structure for morality*. Included in a person's cognitive structure for morality are those moral concepts which that person grasps and the principles incorporating those concepts he or she accepts. As I shall understand it, a principle can be part of one's cognitive structure for morality without one's tending to act on it. You may believe that you ought to speak out against racism and yet, when an acquaintance makes a bigoted remark, prove weak of will. All that is necessary for a principle to belong to your cognitive structure for morality is that you *accept* the principle, that is, believe it. Likewise, in order to belong to a person's cognitive structure for morality, a principle need not be a moral principle. It may, on the contrary, be the denial of a moral principle. If you believe that embezzling is all right if you limit it to modest sums, that principle then belongs to *your* cognitive structure for morality.

Using this concept of a cognitive structure, we can now say that it is a prerequisite of one's internalizing genuinely moral standards—and thus of one's being a moral agent in this world—that one have a cognitive structure for morality. The challenge facing the moral educator is this: How do we bring it about that the child will have a cognitive structure for morality whose principles are both *correct* and *internalized?*

One's cognitive structure for morality might also be regarded as including one's *reasons* for accepting certain standards. A reason for accepting a moral standard will often consist of another, more general moral standard, along with the claim that the one is a special case of the other. (There are other kinds of reasons one might have for accepting a moral standard, but this is the kind we shall focus on in what follows.) "Why do you hold that it is wrong to deceive people?"—"Because I hold that it is wrong to act unlovingly toward people, and that is what I think deception amounts to." To have reasons for one's moral standards is thus to view them as interconnected. It is to see the totality of one's moral standards as something other than a grab-bag of disconnected principles. In offering his summary of the law and the prophets, Jesus taught us that all moral laws are special cases of the law of love.

Must a genuinely moral agent not only have moral standards on which he or she acts but also have good reasons for those standards? Is it necessary to apprehend at least something of the hierarchical structure of the moral law? Certainly this is essential to moral *maturity*. And although we in the West today too easily exaggerate the importance of reasons, we should still say that, if a person had no reasons for any of his or her moral standards and never saw their interconnections, or if his or her reasons were always mistaken, this would certainly mark a lack of moral development. In fact, what we shall see shortly is that even small children, to a quite astounding degree, do have reasons for the standards they affirm.

So once again our question: How does a person acquire (correct) moral standards on which he or she acts? How can the parent or teacher induce in the child the internalization of moral standards? What can be done to bring it about that the principles belonging to the child's cognitive structure for morality are correct and internalized?

In Chapters 9 and 10 we shall look at one phase of this question: How do we lead persons to know their moral obligations? What can we do to bring it about that the standards they accept are truly *moral* standards? In the remainder of this chapter our focus will be on the other phase of our question, the issue of internalization. Suppose that someone has already acquired the moral concepts, presumably by observing others use them, and that he or she already accepts, for example, that embezzling is wrong. How can such a person be induced to tend to *act on* this principle?

From the preceding chapters we know part of the answer. A combination of enunciating a moral standard with physical or social punishment for its violation is effective in causing the person to internalize the standard. We saw that it is not clear just which psychological mechanisms are involved here, but the evidence seems to be that the use of this procedure regularly results in the person's feeling guilt or shame upon violating the standard. The prospect of these "moral emotions" seems to act as a sort of internal monitor. As Bandura says, "People are ordinarily deterred by anticipatory self-censure from engaging in behavior that violates their moral principles. When transgressive behavior is not easily self-excusable, actions are likely to be consonant with moral standards."[2] In any case, instruction supported by discipline is effective in causing internalization.

Also, when a model acts on a moral standard and makes it clear what standard he or she is acting on, and when the model furthermore expresses regret upon violating the standard and satisfaction upon measuring up to it, that too tends to cause internalization of that standard. (It is worth noting here that when we admit our moral failures we not only have an effect on the internalization of the relevant standard by children who observe us. We also teach them how to live with moral imperfection. We model for them how to live obediently with less than perfection.)

[2] *Social Learning Theory*, p. 47.

The presence of articulate moral models in our surroundings—whether "live" or represented makes no appreciable difference—increases the tendency in us to act on those standards. Instruction supported by modeling is effective in causing internalization of standards.

However, one of today's most prominent theories of moral education holds that, although instruction combined with discipline and with modeling may affect the acceptance and internalization of subsidiary standards, it has virtually no effect on the acceptance and internalization of a person's *ultimate* moral reasons, which are acquired in a different way. The theory I have in mind is the Piaget/Kohlberg theory; and we now turn to a detailed examination of the evidence for it and the strategy for moral education recommended by it.

No doubt the popularity of the Piaget/Kohlberg theory can be explained in part by the fact that it goes counter to our preconceptions at many points, making it a striking theory. But it also addresses itself seriously to moral *reasoning*—even, as we shall see, to the point of myopia. And since most research on moral education has been conducted within the orientation of either behaviorism or psychoanalysis, both of which regard the role of reason in human life with profound skepticism, the Piaget/Kohlberg theory has seemed to many like a powerful gust of fresh air blowing away a stale fog. Then, too, Kohlberg presents the strategy of moral education he recommends as itself making no disputable moral commitments; and that has seemed a godsend to public school administrators and teachers in a morally and religiously diverse society.

I shall concentrate on Kohlberg's theory, since it elaborates on and refines Piaget's.[3] The theory of education Kohlberg

[3]What follows is based mainly on Kohlberg's essay "Stages of Moral Development as a Basis for Moral Education," in Beck, Crittenden, & Sullivan (eds.), *Moral Education: Interdisciplinary Approaches* (Univ. of Toronto Press, 1971). The argument in that essay is very much like that in, indeed there are many passages verbally identical with, "From Is to Ought: How to Commit the Naturalistic Fallacy and Get Away with It in the Study of Moral Development," in T. Mischel (ed.), *Cognitive Development and Epistemology* (Academic Press, 1971). I shall also refer to Kohlberg's essay "Continuities in Childhood and Adult Moral Development Revisited" in Baltes & Schaie (eds.), *Life-Span Developmental Psychology: Personality and Socialization* (Academic Press, 1973); and "Develop-

derives from his psychological theory is a specific version of the interaction-developmental ideology discussed in Part One; hence, the reader may wish to review what was said there about that ideology.

Suppose one presents to people a series of moral dilemmas, of which the following (taken from Kohlberg) is a typical example:

> In Europe, a woman was near death from a special kind of cancer. There was one drug that the doctors thought might save her. It was a form of radium that a druggist in the same town had recently discovered. The drug was expensive to make, but the druggist was charging ten times what the drug cost him to make. He paid $200 for the radium and charged $2,000 for a small dose of the drug. The sick woman's husband, Heinz, went to everyone he knew to borrow the money, but he could only get together about $1,000, which is half of what it cost. He told the druggist that his wife was dying and asked him to sell it cheaper or let him pay later. The druggist said, "No, I discovered the drug and I'm going to make money from it." So Heinz got desperate and broke into the man's store to steal the drug for his wife.—Should the husband have done that? Why?

Kohlberg, following Piaget, claims that when a subject is asked about a series of moral dilemmas like this, the *reasons* he or she offers for thinking one course of action should be followed rather than another fall into *patterns*. Two or even more distinct patterns may vie for dominance, but never will there be just a random assortment of reasons. There will always be integrated patterns of moral reasoning.

Kohlberg also claims to have discovered that when we look at the patterns of moral reasoning expressed by different persons, we find very few distinct ones. In fact, from the beginning of his work in the early 1960s until about five years ago,

---

ment as the Aim of Education," in *Harvard Educational Review*, Nov. 1972. A bibliography of Kohlberg's writings by Linda W. Rosenzweig can be found in *Social Education*, Apr. 1976. Many discussions of Kohlberg's work are to be found in the literature. A recent collection which focuses on the relation between Kohlberg's conclusions and religion is Brenda Munsey (ed.), *Moral Development, Moral Education, and Kohlberg* (Religious Education Press, 1980).

Kohlberg claimed that there were only six such patterns. More recently he has suggested that one finds a seventh pattern in a few exceptional individuals and now and then a somewhat disoriented though unique transition pattern in quite a few individuals. But the point remains: patterns of moral reasoning are the common property of humanity, and the distinct items of property are few.

Kohlberg's concern is exclusively with the form of a person's moral reasoning, not the *content*. Two people whose dominant pattern of moral reasoning is identical may choose different courses of action on the moral dilemmas presented to them; conversely, they may agree on *what* should be done but offer distinctly different reasons for doing it.

Kohlberg also claims that when we follow a given person over the years we discover that the person typically goes through a succession of patterns of moral reasoning. At one point in life the dominant reasons given for choosing one rather than another option in a moral dilemma will be of one pattern; later they will be of another. Thus the various patterns of moral reasoning appear in people's lives as *stages*.

If we observe the order in which people typically proceed through stages in their patterns of moral reasoning, we will find, says Kohlberg (in line with interaction-developmental theory generally), that three laws hold: (1) the sequence of stages is invariant for everyone; (2) nobody ever reverts to an earlier stage after having been in a later one; and (3) nobody ever skips a stage.

Because people do move from one stage to another at certain points in their lives, we can offer at least one explanation for their displaying not a single pattern of moral reasoning but rather a dominant pattern along with certain subdominant patterns (or, sometimes, a few *equally* dominant patterns). It is because people are often in transition from pattern to pattern, rather than firmly lodged within one pattern. In their moral reasoning these people will often give evidence both of the stage they are leaving and of the stage they are on the way to.

Another law Kohlberg claims to have discovered is that people *understand* and are attracted to the reasons belonging to the stage next above the one in which they dominantly are, but they do not understand the reasons belonging to stages further above that. If someone *offers* them such reasons for their consideration, they either misconstrue those reasons to fit them into their own dominant stage or the next above, or they just "don't get" what is being said.[4]

Here then, in Kohlberg's own words, are the stages he claims to have discovered:

1. Preconventional level

At this level, the child is responsive to cultural rules and labels of good and bad, right or wrong, but interprets these labels either in terms of the physical or the hedonistic consequences of action (punishment, reward, exchange of favors) or in terms of the physical power of those who enunciate the rules and labels. The level is divided into the following two stages:

Stage 1: *The punishment-and-obedience orientation.* The physical consequences of action determine its goodness or badness, regardless of the human meaning or value of these consequences. Avoidance of punishment and unquestioning deference to power are valued in their own right, not in terms of respect for an underlying moral order supported by punishment and authority (the latter being Stage 4).

Stage 2: *The instrumental-relativist orientation.* Right action consists of that which instrumentally satisfies one's own needs and occasionally the needs of others. Human relations are viewed in terms like those of the marketplace. Elements of fairness, of reciprocity, and of equal sharing are present, but they are always interpreted in a physical, pragmatic way. Reciprocity is a matter of "you scratch my back and I'll scratch yours," not of loyalty, gratitude, or justice.

II. Conventional level

At this level, maintaining the expectations of the individual's family, group, or nation is perceived as valuable in its own right, regardless of immediate and obvious consequences. The attitude is not only one of *conformity* to personal expectations and social order, but of loyalty to it, of actively *maintaining*, supporting, and

---

[4]Kohlberg, "Stages of Moral Development," *loc. cit.*, p. 47.

justifying the order, and of identifying with the persons or group involved in it. At this level, there are the following two stages:

Stage 3: *The interpersonal concordance or "good boy—nice girl" orientation*. Good behavior is that which pleases or helps others and is approved by them. There is much conformity to stereotypical images of what is majority or "natural" behavior. Behavior is frequently judged by intention—"he means well" becomes important for the first time. One earns approval by being "nice."

Stage 4: *The "law and order" orientation*. There is orientation toward authority, fixed rules, and the maintenance of the social order. Right behavior consists of doing one's duty, showing respect for authority, and maintaining the given social order for its own sake.

III. Postconventional, autonomous, or principled level

At this level, there is a clear effort to define moral values and principles that have validity and application apart from the authority of the groups or persons holding these principles and apart from the individual's own identification with these groups. This level also has two stages:

Stage 5: *The social-contract, legalistic orientation*, generally with utilitarian overtones. Right action tends to be defined in terms of general individual rights and standards which have been critically examined and agreed upon by the whole society. There is a clear awareness of the relativism of personal values and opinions and a corresponding emphasis upon procedural rules for reaching consensus. Aside from what is constitutionally and democratically agreed upon, the right is a matter of personal "values" and "opinion." The result is an emphasis upon the "legal point of view," but with an emphasis upon the possibility of changing law in terms of rational considerations of social utility (rather than freezing it in terms of Stage 4 "law and order"). Outside the legal realm, free agreement and contract is the binding element of obligation. This is the "official" morality of the American government and constitution.

Stage 6: *The universal-ethical-principle orientation*. Right is defined by the decision of conscience in accord with self-chosen *ethical principles:* appealing to logical comprehensiveness, universality, and consistency. These principles are abstract and ethical (the Golden Rule, the categorical imperative); they are not concrete moral rules like the Ten Commandments. At heart, these are universal principles of *justice*, of the *reciprocity* and *equality* of human *rights*, and of respect for the dignity of human beings as *individual persons*.[5]

Why do people move from one stage to another? A *necessary* condition of stage advancement which Kohlberg repeatedly emphasizes is growth in intellectual ability. But what might be the sufficient condition? On this Kohlberg's theory is strikingly different from what one would have expected before coming into contact with interaction-developmental theory. One might have expected that people move from one stage to another as the result of being *taught* in one way or another a new and distinct cluster of moral reasons. On Kohlberg's view, such direct teaching can do no more than assist a process which is in its essence fundamentally different. In line with interaction-developmental theory generally, Kohlberg holds that it is a desire to eliminate "cognitive dissonance" (to attain "cognitive equilibrium") that leads to stage advancement.

On this view, each successive stage does a better job of "differentiating" moral concepts from each other and from non-moral concepts and of fitting together its concepts into an "integrated" structure. And so each stage is better able than its predecessors to deal with a broad range of moral problems. Each has more *equilibrium* in the face of moral problems:

These combined criteria, differentiation and integration, are considered by developmental theory to entail a

---

[5] *Ibid.*, pp. 86f., quoting from *Journal of Philosophy*, Oct. 25, 1973. We mentioned above that in one of his recent essays Kohlberg speculates that there may be a seventh "religious" stage, and also that for all or most people who advance to the fifth stage there is an identity crisis "quasi-stage" intervening between the fourth and fifth stages which bears strong surface similarities to the second stage. For these speculations, see his "Continuities in Childhood and Adult Moral Development Revisited" in Baltes & Schaie, *op. cit.*

better equilibrium of the structure in question. A more differentiated and integrated moral structure handles more moral problems, conflicts, or points of view in a more stable or self-consistent way. Because conventional morality is not fully universal and prescriptive, it leads to continual self-contradictions, to definitions of right which are different for Republicans and Democrats, for Americans and Vietnamese, for fathers and sons. In contrast, principled morality is directed to resolving these conflicts in a stable, self-consistent fashion.[6]

Nowhere does Kohlberg state with precision what it means that later stages handle moral problems with more cognitive adequacy. Clearly he does not mean that the stages do a successively better job of getting at what is in fact right or wrong; he is speaking of increasing *cognitive*, not *moral*, adequacy. Perhaps he just means that one stage is more cognitively adequate than another if, for more dilemmas, it yields a clear answer as to what should be done—no matter what the root of that greater clarity. At any rate, Kohlberg (tacitly) postulates in human beings a desire *to achieve cognitive equilibrium;* and that, combined with his claim that successive stages are more cognitively adequate, is a key component in his explanation of stage advancement.[7]

But we are dealing here not with cognitive structures in general but with those which pertain to *moral* problems. To understand such structures, Kohlberg suggests, we must take into account not only the human desire to achieve cognitive equilibrium, but also the human impulse of role-taking. Stages of

---

[6]Kohlberg, "Stages of Moral Development," *loc. cit.*, p. 47.

[7]Kohlberg speaks of the later stages as being more (cognitively) *mature* as well as being more (cognitively) *adequate*. But this is just another way of saying that the later stages have more "differentiation/integration," and thus, on his theory, more "equilibrium." He says, "Both psychological and philosophical analyses suggest that the more mature stage of moral thought is the more structurally adequate. This greater adequacy of more mature moral judgments rests on structural criteria more general than those of truth-value or efficiency. These general criteria are the *formal* criteria developmental theory holds as defining all mature structures, the criteria of increased differentiation and integration" (*ibid.*, p. 46). "Cognitive development is a dialogue between the child's cognitive structures and the structures of the environment" ("Development as the Aim of Education," *loc. cit.*, p. 457).

moral reasoning arise when human beings, given their role-taking impulse, seek to achieve equilibrium in their answers to questions about what to do. Kohlberg says that he, like all his predecessors in interaction-developmental psychology, have "assumed that these stages represent successive modes of 'taking the role of others' in social situations, and hence that the social-environmental determinants of [moral] development are its opportunities for role-taking."[8]

What does Kohlberg mean by this impulse to role-taking? He explains it as the tendency to place oneself in the situation of the other, "the tendency to react to others as like the self and to react to the self's behavior from the other's point of view." It is clear that he understands the impulse to role-taking to have a concern for justice built into it; it is something like *even-handed empathy*. It is not an impulse to take the role of a *particular* other person but to take the role of others equally, impartially, indifferently. "The psychological unity of role-taking and justice at mature stages of moral consciousness is easily recognized."[9] And "if the psychological unity of empathy and justice in moral role-taking is apparent in the stage-6 consciousness ... , it is also apparent at the very start of the moral experience."

> In general, when theorists attempt to extract the culturally universal essence of morality, they turn to (1) rules, (2) sympathy or concern for welfare consequences to

[8]"Stages of Moral Development," *loc. cit.*, p. 42. He states this more elaborately in "From Is to Ought": "A 'cognitive-developmental' theory of moralization is broader than Piaget's own theory, however. By cognitive-developmental I refer to a set of assumptions common to the moral theories of Dewey and Tufts (1932), Mead (1934), Baldwin (1906), Piaget (1932), and myself. All have postulated (a) *stages* of moral development representing (b) *cognitive-structural transformations* in conception of self and society. All have assumed (c) that these stages represent successive modes of '*taking the role of others*' in social situations, and hence that (d) the social-environmental determinants of development are *its opportunities for role-taking*. More generally, all have assumed (e) an *active* child who structures his perceived environment, and hence, have assumed (f) that moral stages and their development represent the *interaction* of the child's structuring tendencies and the structural features of the environment, leading to (g) successive forms of equilibrium in interaction. This equilibrium is conceived as (h) a level of *justice*, with (i) change being caused by disequilibrium, where (j) some optimal level of match or discrepancy is necessary for change between the child and the environment" (*loc. cit.*, pp. 183f.).

[9]"Stages of Moral Development," *loc. cit.*, p. 52.

others, and (3) justice. Developmental theory's conception of role-taking embraces all three, in the sense that all morally relevant rules and institutions are conceived of as interpreted through processes of role-taking directed by concerns about both welfare and justice. All institutions and societies are alike in the sheer fact of being societies, that is, in being systems of defined complementary roles. The primary meaning of the word "social" is the distinctively human structuring of action and thought by role-taking, by the tendency to react to others as like the self and to react to the self's behavior from the other's point of view. Essentially each of our stages defines (or is defined by) a new cognitive-structural mode of role-taking in conflict situations. To understand the development of role taking we must consider not only the principle of empathy or "welfare," considering the effects of action upon the others involved, but also the principle of "justice," that is, of reciprocity and equality in human relations.[10]

The cognitive adequacy of a pattern of reasoning for *moral* issues is its adequacy for dealing with the moral problems confronting a creature with innate role-taking impulses. And in turn, a moral problem "is a conflict between competing claims of men: you versus me, you versus him. The precondition for a moral conflict is man's capacity for role-taking. Most social situations are not moral because there is no conflict in role-taking between the expectations of one person and another."[11]

We must make one more point in exposition of Kohlberg's psychological theory. Kohlberg persistently refers to the stages in their sequence not just as earlier and later, and not just as cognitively less adequate and more adequate, but also as *less advanced morally* and *more advanced morally*. The *principled* Stages, 5 and 6, are the most advanced. One might suppose from this that Kohlberg is judging the principles appealed to in the various stages in terms of their *correctness* and *incorrectness*. It may sound as if Kohlberg regards the justice principle of Stage 6 as the

[10] *Ibid.*, p. 51.
[11] *Ibid.*

most advanced morally because that principle less often than its competitors claims actions to be right which are in fact wrong and vice versa.

But that is not what Kohlberg has in mind. He deliberately avoids speaking of the correctness or incorrectness of these principles or saying that we *ought* to accept certain principles, that we *ought* always to pursue justice, we *ought* always to pursue the greatest happiness of the greatest number, and so on. What he does say is that he does not believe "that moral judgments describe states of the world in somewhat the same way as scientific judgments describe states of the world." Rather, "moral judgments and norms are to be understood ultimately as universal constructions of human actors which regulate their social interaction. . . ."[12] He adds, "We have said that moral judgments are not true or false in the cognitive-descriptivist sense. A higher conception of the value of life or a higher conception of moral emotion . . . is not directly truer than a lower conception."[13]

How is this to be understood? Perhaps Kohlberg's basic point is that it is never right *as such* or wrong *as such* to do something. Instead, actions are only right or wrong *relative to* a certain principle for action. Relative to the justice principle, action X may be wrong; relative to the utility principle, X may be right. We cannot test the principles for correctness by going behind the principles to determine whether the action is right or wrong as such. There is no such thing as choosing an *incorrect* principle, so that if one acts on that principle one does something one ought not to do. All a person can do is apply correctly or incorrectly the principle he or she has chosen. It becomes evident that Kohlberg does not take it to be the ultimate goal of moral education for the student to acknowledge his responsibility. Morality for him is nothing more than a human creation. There is no objective law behind it.

Thus Kohlberg's claim that the principles of Stage 6 are the most adequate morally intends to say nothing about their correctness. Rather, his thought is the following. For a reason to be a truly moral reason, it must by definition appeal to a principle

[12] *Ibid.*, p. 43.
[13] *Ibid.*, p. 48.

which is (1) *universal*, in that it applies to all persons and all actions; (2) *prescriptive*, in that it states what ought to be rather than what is; and (3) *autonomous*, in that it makes no appeal to what anyone else holds on moral matters. On his view, only the principles found at Stage 6 fully satisfy these three formal criteria. Stage 6 is both the most *cognitively adequate* and the *most morally advanced*.

From the foregoing it is easy to infer what Kohlberg does regard as the appropriate goal and strategy of moral education—stage advancement, to the level, one hopes, of the justice principle.

> The goal of moral education is the stimulation of the "natural" development of the individual child's own moral judgment and capacities, thus allowing him to use his own moral judgment to control his behavior. The attractiveness of defining the goal of moral education as the stimulation of development rather than as the teaching of fixed rules stems from the fact that it involves aiding the child to take the next step in a direction towards which he is already tending, rather than imposing an alien pattern upon him.[14]

These comments make it particularly clear that in describing the psychological dynamics at work in moral development, Kohlberg nowhere recognizes any dark side to the human self—no pride, no impulse to self-aggrandizement, no wish to serve oneself at the cost of the other. The human impulses which he sees as relevant to moral development are the impulse to take the role of others and the impulse to seek cognitive equilibrium. From these a commitment to justice will naturally (though not inevitably) grow. Kohlberg apparently recognizes that persons in earlier stages desire to seek their own pleasure, even if it means being indifferent or hostile to the welfare of others; for this appears in the reasons characteristic of the first two stages. But he thinks this impulse is nicely winnowed out by inducing cognitive dissonance in the person, in the face of which he or she will move (if bright enough) to a higher stage, until finally being totally committed to justice. Thus one finds in Kohlberg a classic op-

[14]*Ibid.*, p. 71.

timistic view of humanity and a classic liberal trust in the powers of education.

Kohlberg's *strategy* for achieving the goal of moral education is simple. First, present children moral dilemmas that their stage of moral reasoning is cognitively inadequate to deal with. These may be real-life issues of classroom or society, or hypothetical issues. Encourage the children to decide what should be done and to formulate reasons for thinking so. Second, in the course of their dealing with such dilemmas suggest to them modes of reasoning characteristic of the stage next above their own.

> Facilitating the child's movement to the next step of development involves exposure to the next higher level of thought and conflict requiring the active application of the current level of thought to problematic situations. This implies: (1) attention to the child's mode or styles of thought, i.e., stage; (2) match of stimulation to that stage, e.g., exposure to modes of reasoning one stage above the child's own; (3) arousal, among children, of genuine cognitive and social conflict and disagreement about problematic situations (in contrast to traditional education which has stressed adult "right answers" and has reinforced "behaving well"); and (4) exposure to stimuli toward which the child can be active, in which assimilatory response to the stimulus-situation is associated with "natural" feedback.[15]

There is some evidence that when this strategy is followed for a reasonable length of time, more children advance in stage within that time-span than when this strategy is not followed, though the speed-up is very slight.[16]

Kohlberg never tires of insisting that teachers should concern themselves exclusively with the *form* of a child's moral reasoning, not with the *content*. They should seek to get children to adopt higher patterns of moral reasoning, but not to get them

[15]"Development as the Aim of Education," *loc. cit.*, p. 459.
[16]In his more recent essay, "Continuities in Childhood and Adult Moral Development Revisited," Kohlberg concludes that neither this strategy nor any other classroom strategy is effective in moving students up from Stage 4.

to come to any particular conclusions on moral matters in using that pattern of reasoning. Likewise, Kohlberg never tires of insisting that it is the moral *reasoning* of the student, not *behavior*, which should be of concern in a program of moral education. Form, not content; of reasoning, not of action.

In our search for effective and responsible strategies for inducing persons to internalize moral standards, we have described at length Kohlberg's theory of moral development and its accompanying recommendations for strategy. Kohlberg's work is both psychologically complex and philosophically sophisticated. Now that we have some idea of what he says we shall turn to the assessment of it. First, we should look at the background theory.

An enormous amount of research and controversy has been generated by the claim that there are six or seven integrated patterns of moral reasoning, which occur as stages successive in time. The only thing we can say definitely is that we do not now know whether, or to what extent, the claim is true. Any claim of this type involves deep and complex issues of typology. Its tenability will depend on how one proposes to classify the many diverse responses to the "Why?" questions; and then, having imposed a classification, how one goes about locating a given subject's responses within that classification. Always alternative classifications will be possible; and usually, alternative ways of locating subjects within a classification.[17]

But let us assume some reasonable resolution of these issues. What does then seem to be true is that Stages 1 through 4 are conceptually quite clear, and have some empirical confirmation, whereas by contrast the empirical confirmation for the presence and the order of Stages 5 and 6 is almost nonexistent. That is due in part to the fact that Stages 5 and 6 are much less clear in concept than are the first four. Often one is perplexed as to why Kohlberg fits a sample response under one of these rather than the other. And some responses which seem to be "princi-

---

[17]On this see especially James R. Rest, "New Approaches in the Assessment of Moral Judgment" in Lickona (ed.), *Moral Development and Behavior*. There is also some evidence that when different types of dilemmas are used from those characteristic of Kohlberg's studies, the results are different. See Mussen and Eisenberg-Berg, *op. cit.,* pp. 120ff.

pled" responses apparently fit under neither. For example, it is the biblical proclamation that the ultimate moral law is "you shall love your neighbor as yourself." But surely this is neither a principle of utility nor of equal respect for rights. Where, then, does one fit responses which reflect this understanding of the moral law?

Substantial questions have also been raised about the way Kohlberg explains stage advancement. To get into these controversies here, however, would sidetrack us from our major concerns in these pages. Let it simply be said that, contrary to Kohlberg's thesis, there is evidence that *instruction* and *modeling* account at least in part for a person's being located within a particular stage. It has been discovered, for example, that in some cultures hardly anyone advances beyond Stage 4. Certainly the theory does not lead one to expect that.

Likewise, there is evidence that the different patterns of moral reasoning found in adults in Western society are to some extent correlated with their ideologies, religions, and philosophies. Confirmed utilitarians who express their philosophy in answering the dilemmas will find themselves lodged in Stage 5—but on account of their philosophy, not their drive toward cognitive equilibrium. Those who hold to the divine command theory of ethics and give expression to this theory in responding to the dilemmas will be classified in Stage 4, where Kohlberg puts all those who appeal in any way to authority. But in this instance too it is their theological/philosophical position which accounts for their level, not their desire for cognitive equilibrium in the face of their role-taking impulses. Furthermore, one would expect that those who experience religious conversion will, for quite different reasons from what Kohlberg postulates, shift in their stages of moral reasoning. Not that the desire for cognitive equilibrium and the impulse to role-taking play *no* role in accounting for a person's stage of moral reasoning, but it does seem that these are not the *only* explanatory factors.

Our questions about Kohlberg's background theory raise doubts about the acceptability of an educational strategy which consists of putting that theory to practical application. Even if stage advancement were the proper goal of moral education, the comments just made suggest that other factors are relevant to attaining this goal than those for which Kohlberg allows. But let us be systematic in appraising Kohlberg's educational recommendations, first considering his view that stage advancement is a proper goal for a program of moral education, then weighing his claim that the only effective strategy for speeding up stage advancement is "the Kohlberg strategy," and finally evaluating whether, as he claims, the use of this strategy for this goal is in fact the *only* acceptable program of moral education.

Remember that, on a responsibility theory of education, one's aim in stimulating the development in students of a cognitive structure for morality is for them to wind up with moral standards which are both *internalized* and *correct*, and to have *good* reasons for those standards. The question, then, is whether a program of moral education dedicated to stage advancement is an effective strategy for achieving this.

We should probably assume that people do in fact go through something like Kohlberg's first four stages. And I think we should assume that the reasons characteristic of these stages are *internalized* by people in the stages. Kohlberg's experiments do not in fact tell us that children tend to act on the reasons characteristic of their stage. The experiments tell us only that these are reasons children would *offer* in defense of their views about what ought to be done in certain prospective or hypothetical situations. It seems likely, though, that children are inclined to *act* on the reasons they offer.

But the reasons characteristic of these first four stages are not *correct* ones. The ultimate reason for thinking it right to act in a certain way is *not* that one will thereby bring pleasure to oneself or earn oneself social approval, but that by doing so one will fulfil the demands of love. So none of these first four stages is ultimately acceptable as a cognitive structure for morality.

Accordingly, one should in fact seek to move the child to a higher orientation—up the ladder of the first four stages and then on to an orientation in which the principle of love is the ultimate principle. Assuming that Kohlberg's stage theory is approximately correct for the first four stages,[18] I think that stage ad-

---

[18]As should be clear from my cautious comments, I am not at all confident even of this assumption. I would myself not be surprised if ten years from now, little were left of the Kohlberg conclusions. A good survey of the presently tottery state of Kohlberg's theories is to be found in Howard Munson, "Moral Thinking: Can It Be Taught?" in *Psychology Today*, February, 1979, pp. 48ff.

vancement should in fact be part of the goal of a program of moral education.

The second element in our appraisal of Kohlberg is to ask how such stage advancement is to be promoted. Here we enter an area of less clarity, for, as already remarked, many more factors than those acknowledged by Kohlberg seem to be relevant. There is some evidence, though, that the Kohlberg strategy does in fact slightly speed up the process of stage advancement, up to Stage 4.

The essence of the Kohlberg strategy, beneath all its refinements and accoutrements, is to encourage children themselves to engage in moral reasoning. Instead of *telling* the children that a certain rule is a correct moral standard and offering them reasons for thinking so, one encourages children themselves to settle on some standard by engaging in moral reasoning. Rather than saying, "This is what you should do in this type of situation, and this is why," one encourages children themselves to come up with those conclusions.

That is the heart of the strategy. Its two crucial refinements are these. One presents children with dilemmas, situations in which it will be difficult to figure out what should be done. In these dilemmas reasoning appropriate to a lower stage will prove less cognitively adequate than that appropriate to a higher stage. Then one lures them by suggesting to them the reasons characteristic of a stage higher than that in which they find themselves. If a child is reasoning in terms of the pleasurable and the nonpleasurable, one suggests the possibility of reasoning in terms of social approval and disapproval. If a child is reasoning in terms of preserving the rules of ordered society, one suggests the possibility of reasoning in terms of social utility.

I think that a satisfactory educational program will indeed include situations in which one invites children themselves to engage in moral reasoning. It will not consist merely of handing out do's and don't's. Life inevitably confronts us with many situations in which we must engage in moral reasoning, and education must prepare children for this reality. It will not do so if children are never invited to engage in such reasoning but are merely given the answers. If engaging in the sort of reasoning Kohlberg suggests tends to speed up a child's advance in stage, that is certainly a benefit. And it appears that it does in fact do so—provided that children are confronted with cases which they find hard to handle in their current mode of thinking, and provided that a better way of handling them is suggested. The dilemmas on which one invites children to reflect may be either hypothetical or actual situations from school, home, or society.

So stage advancement is an appropriate goal of moral education, and Kohlberg's strategy of encouraging children to "cut their teeth" on moral dilemmas may, among other benefits, cause stage advancement to occur somewhat more quickly. Now we must turn to the third part of our analysis of Kohlberg. Is it true, as Kohlberg insists, that moral education should aim at *nothing else* than stage advancement, and that the *only* strategy used for achieving this goal should be the one he proposes?

In fact these insistences are based on little else than liberal bias. In defense of them, Kohlberg says that using this strategy for this goal "does not entail the violation of the child's moral freedom, which is involved in any other formulation of moral education goals. . . . The legitimacy of the developmental approach to moral education is that the stimulation of moral development defines an educational process respecting the autonomy of the child, whereas any other definition reflects indoctrination."[19] Explaining what he means by "indoctrination," Kohlberg says that "the experiences by which children naturally move from stage to stage are nonindoctrinative, that is, they are not experiences of being taught and internalizing specific content." And again, promoting the adoption of "such principles is nonindoctrinative if these principles are not presented as formulae to be learned ready-made or as rote patterns grounded in authority."[20]

These remarks are rife with confusion. Kohlberg constantly works with the metaphor of *form* and *content*. On his view, the teacher may promote advancement in the *form* of moral reasoning, since that is merely speeding up the natural process, but with respect to *content* there is apparently no natural process; hence, the teacher should keep "hands off." But as we saw ear-

---

[19]"Stages of Moral Development," *loc. cit.*, pp. 71f.
[20]"Development as the Aim of Education," *loc. cit.*, p. 475.

lier, a *reason* for a moral standard is nothing but *another*, more general, moral standard, along with the claim that the standard *for which* a reason is given is a special case of the standard contained in the reason. Thus a Kohlbergian teacher is not promoting the adoption by the student of an empty "form," but the adoption of a highly general *moral standard*.

Further, it is not true that any "content" whatever can be poured into a given "form," nor that anyone thinks it can. A person who is committed above all to the law-and-order of society will come to different conclusions on many issues from someone committed to personal pleasure, and from someone committed to equal respect for rights. True, those committed above all to law-and-order will not all come to the same conclusion on every issue. But unless they are terribly benighted, they will certainly come to the same conclusion on *many* issues. Thus the teacher who seeks to move a child to Stage 4 reasoning is in fact thereby seeking to get him or her to accept a whole range of relatively specific moral standards—in addition to that totally general standard of law-and-order as being ultimately right. Kohlberg has no scruples against seeking to induce children to commit themselves to the totally general moral principle of equal respect for human rights. But this implies that he should also have no scruples against seeking to induce those children to commit themselves to a whole range of applications of that principle. For in fact he cannot do the first without also doing the second, since many of the applications are perfectly obvious.

But if that is so, then what possible ground could there be for insisting that the teacher not help the student apply the general principle to cases which are not obvious—the difficult and ambiguous ones? Kohlberg sometimes speaks as if he thinks that the only way to promote the acceptance by others of specific moral standards (content) is to use operant conditioning. He makes clear that he opposes the use of this technique for that purpose. But we have seen that that is *not* the only way. For one thing, by inducing the acceptance (and internalization) of a highly general moral standard one also induces the acceptance (and internalization) of its obvious applications. And secondly one can *show* someone how a general principle applies to non-obvious cases and *thereby* induce the acceptance (and internalization) of standards for these cases. (We will be looking more at this in the next chapter.)

But apart from this, why is it always wrong to use operant conditioning to induce a child's acceptance (and internalization) of a moral standard? Operant conditioning can scarcely be avoided, but even when it can be avoided, why is it invariably wrong? Praise and blame work (in part) by way of operant conditioning. Is it always wrong to praise and chastise? Kohlberg himself seems not to think so, for he writes in a recent essay that "praise and blame are necessary parts of moral development."[21]

In summary, part of the teacher's goal is for the child to internalize correct moral standards. One strategy for achieving that is apparently the Kohlbergian strategy. Another strategy is the enunciation of standards in combination with discipline for the violation of those standards. A third strategy is the enunciation of standards by models who act on those standards. Though we are far from knowing how these strategies are best combined, we do know that the Kohlbergian strategy is ineffective for inducing a child to move beyond Stage 4. Thus it is ineffective for causing the child to internalize *correct* moral standards (since those which define Stages 1 through 4 are not correct). To achieve that, some combination of moral instruction with discipline and modeling is apparently required. So far as we can tell, that strategy will involve the attachment of the moral emotions (guilt, shame, and the like) to the violation of those standards and will thus contribute to their internalization.

If Kohlberg's insistence that we focus on the form and not the content of a child's moral reasoning is groundless, his insistence that we focus on the child's reasoning rather than action is simply strange. After all, what is moral reasoning for, if not action? True, in recent essays Kohlberg has begun to claim that the more advanced a person is in moral reasoning, the more likely it is that he or she will act morally. But he still treats moral action as a *benefit* of advancement in reasoning, rather than as the *goal* for the sake of which such advancement is pursued.

It would be pointless to belabor this myopic concern of Kohlberg with patterns of reasoning as opposed to tendencies of

[21]"Stages of Moral Development," *loc. cit.*, p. 77.

action. But the presence and sequence of the stages do raise some perplexing questions for the parent or teacher who is concerned with action. Let me, in conclusion, say a word about these.

One may presumably infer that a person in Stage 1 is motivated in moral situations largely by the prospect of getting rewards and avoiding punishments; a person in Stage 2 by the prospect of enjoying the pleasant and avoiding the unpleasant; in Stage 3 by the prospect of social approval and the avoidance of disapproval; in Stage 4 by the prospect of what would conform to the rules of his or her society and the will of its authorities. The Kohlberg experiments do not, of course, *tell us* that the reasons characteristic of these stages do in fact tap the motivational structure of the child, but only that these are the reasons which would be offered in defense of the chosen solutions to various moral dilemmas. Yet it seems likely that the subjects are also expressing what would motivate them in such situations.

Seen in this light, the first four Kohlberg stages can be viewed as displaying in succession the relative effectiveness of various types of reinforcers the child experiences. Moving as it does, roughly from the physical to the social, the sequence has nothing at all surprising about it: it is exactly what one would expect. Kohlberg's first four stages appear to refer to various desirable and undesirable consequences of our actions; and their sequence appears to show the sequence of those expectations concerning the external consequences of our actions which are effective in motivating the child. In short, there seems to be an intimate connection between these Kohlberg stages and our discussion of conditioning in Chapter 5.

Suppose, then, that one wishes to get a Stage 3 child to return some lost article which he or she has found, thus to act in accord with the moral law. Since the child is in Stage 3, we know that praise and blame, social approval and disapproval, will be particularly effective reinforcers. Eventually, indeed, we hope that the tendency to return lost articles to their owners will become internalized. But until it is (and even when it is) there is nothing wrong in the use of social reinforcers.

But does one, in addition to using these social reinforcers, say that the child *ought* to return the article *because* people will think better of him or her? Does one cite that as a reason for its being the *right* thing to do? Is *that* an appropriate use of our knowledge of the stages? Kohlberg would apparently never use the stages this way. But that is because he resists using reasons to get the child to act in a certain way. The truth, indeed, is that he resists cultivating tendencies to action in the child no matter how one does so. All such activity he regards as unwarranted imposition by adults on children.

Do we who wish to cultivate in children a tendency to act in a certain way, however, offer them Stage 3 reasons as to why it is right to return lost articles? After all, the reason it is *right* to return them is *not* that people will then approve. The ultimate moral standard is not "Whatever is likely to win us social approval is right." Do we nonetheless reason with the child on his or her own level? Do we accommodate ourselves to children's moral misconceptions, assuming that they will eventually emerge from darkness into the light of true morality? Until children do come out of the moral gloom of the first four stages, do we never offer as a reason for their *obligations* to action that they will thereby display consideration for their neighbors or respect for their neighbors' rights?

Most emphatically one ought not to proceed thus. Make use, indeed, of the reinforcers that seem effective. But do not say to the child that the reason one *ought* to return a lost article is that people will then think better of one. It may be true that people will; if so, fine. A child's knowledge of that can then function as a motive for doing it, and there is no harm in citing that motive. But it is not a reason for its being *right* to do so. Honesty may in fact pay. One's awareness that it pays may motivate one to be honest. But the *reward* for honesty is not the reason that it is *right* (obligatory) to be honest. And what could be the point of saying to anybody, even to children, that it is?

Then, too, reasons come in a hierarchy, as we have seen. One need not always cite the *ultimate* moral reason to the child. "It belongs to Joe. It doesn't belong to you. We shouldn't take things that don't belong to us, or keep them if we know whose they are." In such a snatch of conversation the speaker cites a genuinely moral principle, one which the child perhaps understands. It is not, indeed, the *ultimate* moral standard. But it is not necessary that the child understand just how this all fits with the law of love. I have suggested, on the contrary, that moral *maturity* consists in coming to grasp the hierarchical structure of the moral law. Kohlberg's myopic preoccupation with a child's *ultimate* standards yields a quite misleading picture of the moral life.

9

One More Strategy: Casuistry

In Chapters 5 and 6 we looked at two grand strategies for cultivating tendencies to act in accord with the moral law—discipline and modeling. In Chapter 7 we considered how such tendencies can most effectively be internalized. Punishment apparently has some effect, by way of attaching the negative moral emotions to violations; but what is most effective is discipline and modeling combined with the presentation of reasons for acting in the way desired, reasons such that the standard incorporated in the reason is one on which the child will act. Then in Chapter 8 we looked at some of the ways a person can be encouraged to accept and act on moral standards.

For all this there is evidence in the psychological literature, though as we saw there is more at some points than others. In this chapter we shall go beyond the psychological literature to look at another extremely important strategy for cultivating in children (and others) internalized tendencies to act in accord with the moral law.[1] To name this strategy I shall resurrect the old word "casuistry." The unsavory connotation most people attach to this word is that of trying to get out of doing what you know perfectly well to be your duty by discovering some subtlety in the case from which you argue that it is not your duty after all. But casuistry in the original sense in which we use it here is simply the attempt to apply general moral principles to perplexing cases, thus to find out what *ought to be done in such instances*.

---

[1]Possibly the evidence concerning the effects of sustained "preaching" is relevant here. It has been shown that the long-term effects of direct and rather expansive "preaching" are just as strong as those of modeling. See Grusec, Saas-Kortsaak, and Simutis, "The Role of Example and Moral Exhortation in the Training of Altruism," in *Child Development*, 49 (1978), 920–23. Compare Mussen and Eisenberg-Berg, *loc. cit.*, pp. 151ff.

Casuistry is exactly the form of moral reasoning which the teacher invites the students to practice in the Kohlberg strategy. My suggestion here is that one strategy for cultivating moral tendencies in children and others, with respect to a case in which they have no very definite tendencies, is to present them with a specimen of moral reasoning, showing how the general principles they accept and tend to act on apply to this more specific—and often perplexing—case. One could say that the parent or teacher in such a situation is engaged in moral reasoning with the child, but speaking thus would constantly invite confusion with the Kohlberg strategy, in which it is the children themselves who engage in the reasoning. This is why I have introduced the term "casuistry," hoping that its unsavory connotations can be shucked off.

The exercise of casuistry by the teacher with the students ought to be one of the most prominent strategies in a complete program of moral education. Presenting people specimens of this sort of moral reasoning is one of the most important devices for cultivating in them internalized tendencies to act in accord with the moral law. All of us have been in situations in which we have been puzzled about what we should do. We have read books or articles or listened to speakers on the matter in question and reflected on it ourselves. Such reading, listening, and reflection have helped us come to see how the general principles to which we were already committed apply to this perplexing situation. And sometimes, at least, we have then gone off to act accordingly. An internalized tendency has been developed in us, by our participation in a specimen of casuistry.

The young American men during the Vietnam War who were perplexed as to their duty read books and articles and listened to speeches of casuistry—or engaged in it themselves. Bankers who try to determine whether it is their moral duty to withdraw funds under their control from South Africa read or listen to casuistry—or engage in it themselves. General moral principles about justice and obligations to one's neighbor and the duties of citizenship need to be brought to bear on these specific and perplexing issues.

Surrounded by specimens of casuistry, we all engage in it ourselves to some extent. It is an indispensable part of our moral existence, and sometimes it seems to "work." Yet the psycholog-ical literature has ignored it. Since it does sometimes contribute to the cultivation of internalized tendencies to act in accord with the moral law, I propose that we acknowledge it as an indispens-able part of moral education.

The difference between this and the Kohlberg strategy is worth emphasizing once more. When I say that casuistry should be an important part of moral education, I do not mean that we should simply set a moral problem before our children and let them "cut their teeth" on it. We should not just let them *practice* casuistry, play at it. That is the essence of the Kohlberg strategy. That strategy has a place, but here I am recommending that parents and teachers actually try to show children the implica-tions of certain general moral standards for special types of cases, about which children feel more or less bewildered. My proposal is not that we just teach children how to go about applying general moral standards to special sorts of perplexing situations, but that we *do actually apply* the general standards to some such situations and contribute in that way to cultivating internalized tendencies to act in accord with the moral law. My proposal is that casuistry be used to give moral guidance. Of course, presenting children with seriously intended specimens of casuistry will also have the important benefit of teaching them how to engage in such moral reasoning on their own.

But casuistry by itself will do no good. If the student does not accept and act on the general moral principles which are relevant to a specimen of casuistry, showing how they apply will normally have no effect on inculcating the relevant tendency. Thus the workings of casuistry *presuppose* moral knowledge and commitment—internalized moral standards—on the part of the child.

Can casuistry be used with small children, if Kohlberg's stage theory is anywhere near correct? The Kohlberg theory claims, for example, that a Stage 2 person tries to handle moral problems by considerations of pleasure and pain. But the princi-ple "What gives pleasure is right to do and what gives pain is wrong to do" is not, of course, a (correct) *moral* principle. Does it not then follow from the Kohlberg experiments that people who are not yet beyond Stage 4 have no internalized general moral standards to which the strategy of casuistry can appeal? No doubt casuistry is more appropriate with adults and adolescents than small children. But we would be falling into confusion if we concluded, on the basis of the Kohlberg studies, that it has no application to children. What we learn from the Kohlberg experiments (if their conclusions are correct) is that children are mistaken in what they take as their *most ultimate* principle. What they offer as their ultimate reason is not, in fact, the correct ultimate moral principle. But they may, nonetheless, be correct on a good many other, less ultimate, principles. They may believe, for example, that lying is wrong. And they would be right on that— for most cases, anyway. The fact that they may be mistaken in their ultimate reason for thinking lying is wrong does not mean that they are mistaken in the principle that lying is wrong. And this, then, is something to which the casuist can appeal.

Casuistry then works within the framework of prior knowledge and commitment. It presupposes at least the beginnings of a correct and internalized cognitive structure for morality. Even then it will not always work. A person may tend to act on some general moral standard and have internalized it. Yet when he or she is shown that this general principle definitely applies to situations of a certain sort, the anticipated results of acting on the general principle in a particular instance may be too frightening. To follow through an earlier example, a young American in the late 1960s who wanted to act on his own internalized moral standards about when participation in a war is just may clearly have come to the conclusion that he ought to refuse his draft call. Yet the consequences of doing so—the degradation of prison or the loneliness of exile to Canada or Sweden—may have been too much for him to face, so that he did not in fact refuse induction. Casuistry is not an all-sufficient technique for cultivating internalized tendencies—but neither is anything else.

How does the strategy of casuistry proceed? It will always involve a situation of a certain kind about which one wonders what ought to be done. One may be genuinely in the dark as to what should be done; or one may have strong hunches as to what is morally required, without seeing why it is required and—on the chance that one's hunches are mistaken—want to discover the relevant principles. We can distinguish six phases of casuistic discussion:

1. Describe the facts of the situation as accurately as possible and as elaborately as necessary. Although this sounds easy enough, the root of many of our moral perplexities is often right here. A moral standard which is clearly of direct relevance to the question of abortion is "you shall not kill." But disputes rage over whether the life of a *person* is being taken in every case of abortion. It is the facts which are in dispute. Similarly, governments often deliberately keep from their citizens factual information relevant to a given person's decision as to whether obedience to this or that law would be moral.

2. Try to discover the various options actually available to the agent. Always one will be confronted with a choice. Specify the possible choices.

3. Decide whether some of these options are already clearly ruled out by moral law. Usually some are. Perhaps one of the choices involves complicity in an illegal and immoral price-fixing scheme.

4. Try to predict the consequences of each of the remaining options.

5. Decide which of one's moral standards seem to apply to the case as thus outlined. Is it a case of misleading someone? Is it also a case of saving someone's life? Is it a case of disobedience to duly constituted authority?

6. If necessary, decide which of the standards that apply ought to receive priority. The Dutch in wartime who undertook to hide Jews repeatedly had to decide whether their responsibility to protect human life overrode their responsibility not to deceive.

Of course, the process of casuistry would be absurdly wooden if one insisted that these phases must always be kept sharply distinguished or that they must always be taken up in the order given. These are—to repeat it—distinguishable phases of casuistic discussion. And sometimes one of these *phases* will be the source of the moral uncertainty, sometimes another.

10

Some Qualifications and Applications

Characteristic of modern liberal thought concerning morality is the insistence that nobody should ever adopt any moral standard *on authority*. Nobody should ever take anybody's word for it on moral matters. Nobody should ever make a moral decision on somebody else's advice. Everybody should become autonomous.

We saw this attitude emerging in what Kohlberg said about his "principled" level of morality, Stages 5 and 6, which he regards as the level which is most adequate morally. A person at this level appeals to principles which are universal, prescriptive, and *autonomous*. Apparently what he means by this last qualifier is that the principles accepted incorporate no reference to someone's say-so, and that the person's reason for accepting whatever principles he or she does is likewise never someone's say-so.

Notice how absurd it would be to insist on this sort of autonomy in other areas of life. Most people constantly appeal to authority. Few of us would think of searching through the medical literature to find out about physical symptoms we are experiencing; we consult a physician whom we trust. But morality, the modern liberal tells us, must be treated differently. In morality one should never take anybody's word for it. Stated briefly, the usual argument for this view is that in morality there is nothing to be *known*. Either there is nothing for anybody's word to be about; or, if there is, everybody's word is as good as anybody else's, since in morality we can never get beyond belief to knowledge.

The advice is ridiculous, and fortunately hardly anybody ever follows it. Almost all of us go for advice on moral matters to people whom we regard as wise—to parents, pastors, trusted friends, grandparents, teachers. We put to them our perplexities, and they respond by saying such things as "I think that what should count above all in such cases is . . . , so I would advise you to. . . ." Or, "Almost always what I've seen happen in such cases is . . . , so I would advise you to. . . ." We often take their word for it. We follow their advice without ourselves insisting on duplicating the reflection or experience which taught them this. Almost everyone in fact appeals to moral authorities; the only exceptions are the fiercely independent and the intellectually liberal.

This is as it should be, for some people have a better grasp of the moral law and its applications than others. In general, parents and teachers have a better grasp of it than small children. True, all of us probably have to engage in casuistry at some time in our lives in order to figure how the general principles to which we are committed apply to some case in which we don't quite know what to do. But some of us are better at casuistry than others. Some of us have more time for it than others. And it is appropriate for those of us who are not very skilled at it, or who lack the time for it, to go to someone whose commitments and insight we have come to respect, and take his or her word for it. And even for those who have the time and skill for detailed casuistry, appeal to moral authority remains relevant. We simply do not have time to figure everything out for ourselves. We do not even have time for every moral issue that comes our way, either to figure it out for ourselves or to follow the detailed moral reasoning of someone who has figured it out. Surely taking up the slack by following the advice of someone whom we respect as a moral authority is better than just doing what one feels like doing.

To put the issue more precisely, an appeal to authority in moral matters means one of two quite different things—as does the insistence that we should all become autonomous. Some hold that the obligatory is what some authority wills; the authority's willing it is what makes it right. This is a view concerning the ontological status of moral law. A second view is that some persons know better than others what the moral law requires on certain matters; in fact they know well enough for us to "trust their authority." This is a view concerning our *knowledge* of the moral law. No doubt Kohlberg, like Western liberals in general, wants to say that authority has nothing to do either with the ontological status of moral law or with our mode of knowing it.

They want to say that we should accept only autonomous principles, and that all our acceptance of principles should be autonomous.

This view conflicts with what Christians hold concerning the status of the moral law. Christians believe the moral law to be the will and command of a loving God. To be sure, a person can apprehend parts of the moral law without acknowledging its status as being what God commands. Yet authority has a central part in the Christian understanding of the very status of moral law. And, of course, Christians believe that the moral law is objective. There *is* something there to be known.

But more than this, Christians hold that this same God who ties us to himself by cords of responsibility also *speaks* to us. In the course of this speech he *informs* us of his will for our lives and *instructs* us in his moral law. He does this centrally, though not exclusively, in the Scriptures of the Old and New Testaments. So the Christian holds that there is among us a decisive moral authority—the Scriptures. Concerning moral matters we do indeed "take it on someone's word"—on Isaiah's word, for instance, and on John's word—because in their words we hear God speaking. Not that no one else may ever be consulted on moral matters. But for Christians the Scriptures are authoritative, and growth in the moral life includes taking them as authoritative.

But the Bible is not a moral answer book for all the issues that come our way in the course of twentieth-century existence. As the record of God's dealings with his ancient chosen people—first Israel, then his own Son, then the early church—and of their response to his dealings with them, the Bible comes in many forms: letters, gospels, historical accounts, temple songs, wisdom literature. Sometimes it is perfectly obvious how its message applies to your and my twentieth-century moral situation, but that is not always so. Thus we need instruction in how to use it properly, how to respect its integrity while at the same time taking it as genuinely authoritative for our lives. We must learn how to apprehend the general principles which underlie what it says, and then we must combine those discoveries with casuistry in order to make application to our own lives. Moral education within a program of Christian education must give a prominent role to teaching the students how to discover the authoritative message of the Scriptures for their lives.

*   *   *

It will be useful at this point to review briefly what I have suggested concerning responsible and effective strategies for moral education.

To be a moral agent is to act *in accord with* the moral law. But in our world it is not only that: it is also, for a wide range of cases, to *act on* a principle which coincides with the moral law (and not to act on principles which conflict with the moral law). Parents and teachers cannot guarantee that children will act in such a manner. What they can do is to cultivate the tendency to act in accord with the moral law. Likewise they can cultivate the acceptance of principles which coincide with the moral law and on which the child tends to act, along with helping children apprehend good reasons for their principles. These last two points can be combined by saying that a cognitive structure for morality can be cultivated in students which coincides with the moral law and is internalized by them. Morality has a behavioral dimension and a cognitive or intellectual dimension, distinguishable but interlocked. (Likewise it has, as we have seen, an emotional dimension.)

A tendency to act in accord with the moral law can be cultivated in someone by appropriate use of both discipline and modeling. But what appears to be the best way to *internalize* such a tendency is for a person who acts lovingly toward the child to combine discipline and modeling with the enunciation of a moral standard which the child perceives to fit the situations and on which he or she is willing to act (that is, to internalize). What seem especially effective are reasons in which the adult invites the child to take the role of the other and consider how that person would feel.

Conversely, one of the ways to cultivate the internalization of a moral standard is to combine its enunciation with discipline and with articulate modeling. The apparent effect of combining the enunciation of a moral standard with punishment (physical and social) for violating it is to evoke feelings of guilt or shame upon violation of the standard; and that plays a role in the development of the internal monitor of conscience. There is also some evidence in the Kohlberg experiments that children move through a series of unsatisfactory ultimate standards before they are ready to adopt genuinely moral ultimate standards, and that this natural developmental process can be speeded up by confronting the student with "tough cases," while at the same time suggesting the use of a standard higher up the scale. Finally, the practice of what we called casuistry is often effective in cultivating internalized tendencies and, of course, in cultivating internalized lower-level standards.[1]

But how do teachers and students acquire a *knowledge* of this moral law which is to be internalized in the form of standards to be acted on? In this book I have not attempted a general account of the nature of moral *knowledge* and how we acquire it (what one might call an epistemology of morality). But I have said that for all of us casuistry plays a fundamental role in the acquisition of (lower-level) knowledge of how we ought to act; and that it is the Christian conviction that God, in the Scriptures, speaks authoritatively to our moral obligations.

These conclusions will provoke diverse reactions. Many will be profoundly annoyed by the assumption that there is an objective moral law, which has the status of God's command for our lives. Many teachers will no doubt be disappointed that little by way of objectives for lesson plans has emerged. "But what can I *teach*? What textbooks can I use? What work can I assign? What lectures can I prepare? Where's a good program that I can follow?" Parents, practicing, as they mainly do, informal education, will perhaps quite readily grasp the point that it is various dimensions of their comportment—the dimensions to which we have called attention—which serve to shape the tendencies of their children. But teachers want curricula.

---

[1]Though the evidence is not so very decisive, one more strategy is worth mentioning in a footnote. At least for certain kinds of moral actions it helps to assign the child responsibility. See the review in Mussen and Eisenberg-Berg, *Roots of Caring, Sharing, and Helping,* pp. 97–99, 155.

The fundamentals of moral education do not constitute material for lesson plans but advice on how teachers should comport themselves. To acknowledge this will require a fundamental reorientation on the part of many teachers. Yet the point must not be exaggerated either. There *is* some material to be taught. The application of general principles to specific cases—what we call casuistry—is lesson-plan material. Instructing the child in the proper use of the Bible is lesson-plan material. And (though in my judgment this is much less important) there is room in lesson plans for Kohlbergian exercises. But the main point remains: Moral education overflows the lesson plans of teachers into their lives. Like all of us, teachers teach by how they live and act.

Thus in order to teach morality, the school must itself be a moral community. More generally, to teach the Christian way of life, the school must itself exhibit that way of life. It must be a community of peace, *shalom*, love. Of course, the desire to teach what it aims to teach is not the only reason for the school to seek to be a community of love. The Christian school is the body of Christ coming to expression in a certain locale, there and then. Moral action is important for the present, not just the future, for life in that classroom, not just life outside, for that teacher and those children, not just for others. The joy and peace in human relations which moral action brings should be present in each classroom—for its inherent worth, not just for its instructional benefits.

Let me take note here of an important limitation on this discussion. We have discussed an array of responsible and effective strategies for educating children morally. But it would be nice also to know which of these strategies, used in which manner, is most effective for a given level of maturity. We know that the child is in the process of maturing, and it seems likely that not all of the strategies suggested work equally well at every level of maturity. Since effective teaching always takes account of the student's level of maturity, we would like to know the details as to which strategies work best for which level, handled in which way. We would like to see our conclusions placed within the context of an articulate theory of child development.

To undertake that project responsibly, with care and thoroughness, is a sizeable task. Here and there I have made some remarks relevant to it, but as a whole it falls outside the limits of this essay. I hope this discussion will stimulate those knowledgeable in the field to take up the challenge.[2] Meanwhile, the conclusions I have drawn will have to be applied with common sense, plus whatever theoretical knowledge the teacher may have acquired concerning the development of children.

*   *   *

Anyone who undertakes to speak carefully and thoughtfully about moral education must do so, as we said at the outset, in the light of contemporary psychological evidence and theories. I have sought to do that in the foregoing. But having made use of the psychological literature in arriving at strategies for moral education, I want to conclude with some warnings.

We must be cautious, in the first place, about the significance we attach to conclusions drawn from the evidence. The most that any of the strategies I have recommended can do is increase the likelihood that certain results will occur. They cannot guarantee them. We know how to *cultivate* the formation of a moral agent, but not how to *guarantee* it. In my judgment, that is because there *is* no way. Most of the conclusions of the psychological research reflect a determinism on this score. The reason we cannot assure the formation of a moral agent is thought to be that we do not know enough of the crucial variables, or that when we do occasionally know them, we cannot gain control over them.

Surely it is true that we do not know all the crucial variables. But people are *free agents*—if not with respect to everything they do, probably with respect to most of what they do. They are created capable of *choosing* to a great extent which motives they will act on, which standards they will adopt as reasons for their actions, which goals they will pursue. Often a person can act otherwise than he or she does without violating any causal law. Of course their choices are made in the light of their

---

[2]Some of the relevant evidence can be found in the book by P. Mussen and N. E. Eisenberg-Berg cited in the previous note.

knowledge of all sorts of things happening *to* them and *within* them. Thus even in their freedom they are capable of being influenced. Furthermore, we can adopt strategies for influencing other people which attempt to circumvent their knowledge and freedom. Yet all but the most severely disturbed persons remain free. And so it is that the formation of a moral agent cannot be guaranteed.

Another caution must be issued concerning how we use the conclusions from the psychological evidence. Let me begin with an analogy. Scientists have learned a great deal about the human body's need for vitamins. That knowledge apparently constitutes a powerful temptation for Americans to counteract their habit of eating junk foods by popping pills which (so the scientists assure us) contain all the vitamins necessary. It has not led them to discontinue eating junk foods. In this way a scientific discovery is put to technological use. But what repeatedly happens is that scientists discover in natural foods trace-vitamins and trace-minerals which prove to be essential to good health. The moral is obviously to eat natural foods, not junk foods plus pills, and to use the scientific knowledge as a guide in one's choice of those natural foods.

How does this relate to what we have been discussing? Psychologists have discovered various facts about what contributes to the formation of a moral agent. They and their followers are then constantly tempted to construct highly artificial situations in which to put to technological use *their* particular discoveries. Thus one gets Kohlberg's program, in which one attends solely to advancing the "form" of a child's pattern of moral reasoning. Thus one gets that grotesque behaviorist vision of the school of the future in which the child is manipulated from 9 until 3 with the promise of sugar plums and the threat of "No gym today." But we simply do not know enough—and probably never will know enough—to justify the use of these moral analogies to the junk food/pill popping strategy. Parents and teachers must be told to use these discussions of the psychologists as guidelines to their natural loving interaction with the child. In that natural interaction there are bound to be "traces" of beneficial elements as yet undiscovered by the most creative of researchers.

Some cautionary words ought also to be said about the character of the evidence itself and how conclusions are drawn from it. Obviously it is often unclear what generalization should be drawn from a body of experiments, since it is unclear what the crucial variables are. Thus all the conclusions should, in varying degrees, be treated as tentative. A less obvious but possibly more important point is this: on the basis of experiments conducted from within a number of different psychological orientations, I have made recommendations concerning strategies. I have done so without the guidance of a unified psychological theory—or to put it in other words, without an articulated psychological model of man. Instead, I have followed the theological/philosophical image of man presented in Part One and my understanding of the nature of the moral agent. With that image of man and that understanding, it was necessary to pick and choose, for the orientations which have inspired the experiments on moral education are all reductionistic, each fixing on *one* phase of the human moral life to the neglect of the others.

No other procedure seems possible at this point, yet it is dangerous to pick and choose in the psychological literature without oneself having a general explanatory theory. One danger is that the strategies one recommends will add up to nothing more than a disconnected hodgepodge. I hope to have circumvented this danger. Our theological/philosophical image of man and our understanding of the moral agent seem to have guided us to an array of strategies which fit together.

But there is another danger, which is much more difficult to avoid, in picking and choosing among experiments conducted within a variety of psychological orientations without oneself having a comparable psychological orientation as guide. That is the danger of unwittingly accepting the distortions induced by those orientations. An illustration of this is the dispute between the radical behaviorists (like B. F. Skinner) and the social learning theorists (like Albert Bandura). Bandura by no means discards as worthless all the experiments of the behaviorists, but in the light of his own theory that human behavior is mainly determined by expected rather than actual consequences, he describes the results of those experiments differently, he sometimes raises questions about their design, he attaches different significance to them, and he himself pursues quite different lines of experimentation. The same thing happens to someone who has an articulated psychological model of man faithful to the theological/philosophical image and understanding of the moral agent presented here. Perhaps few of the experiments will be discarded as worthless, but many will be seen in quite a different light.

Each of us can do no more than operate in the situation in which we find ourselves. What I have done in this book is only a precarious introduction. I hope it will stimulate Christian psychologists to articulate a psychological model of the human being faithful to the Christian vision, and then in the light of that model to sift through the available evidence on moral education and themselves acquire evidence where evidence is lacking. To put it that way is to put it misleadingly, however. One doesn't *first* have the model all worked out and *then* look at the evidence. One's formation of a model and one's sifting through the evidence—all the while trying to be faithful to the Christian image of man—occur together. They go on simultaneously.

One final word of caution. To give some order to my discussion I have taken up various phases of the moral life in succession—first the inculcation of tendencies, then the internalization of tendencies, then the internalization of standards, and so on. No one should assume that actual moral education must follow the order of our discussion here. Usually the various phases will occur simultaneously.

*　　　　　*　　　　　*

My overarching aim in this essay has been to discover and suggest responsible and effective strategies for cultivating tendencies to action, ranging from unreflective habits to highly self-conscious commitments. I suggested that anyone who adopts a responsibility theory of education will consider it one of the teacher's responsibilities to cultivate various tendencies in the child, thus to be concerned with tendency learning. Those teachers who are reluctant to include tendency learning among their educational goals—who want to stick with the cultivation of knowledge and abilities—should reflect on the fact that teachers unavoidably influence the tendencies of their students anyway.

Though tendency learning in general has been my concern in this book, I have focused on moral education in Part Two, because most of the research in tendency learning has focused on moral education. But the lessons learned in moral education can be applied to other tendency learning. If the school is concerned to train and equip for responsible action generally, it will have to be concerned not only with the moral aspects of life but also the political aspects, the aesthetic and artistic, the recreational, the economic, the ecological, and so on. How can we apply what we have learned to these other aspects?

It would be outside the purpose of this book—not to mention tedious—to discuss any of these other areas in detail. Let me then take the area of ecological responsibility as an example and show briefly how what we have learned about moral education can be applied to other aspects of life.

Our goal in educating for ecologically responsible action will include two comprehensive and connected elements. We want to develop in children internalized tendencies to act in accord with their responsibilities to the environment. And we want to develop in them an internalized cognitive structure for ecologically responsible action, so that they will recognize their responsibilities to the environment and tend to act on that recognition. How can we accomplish this?

As always, discipline will have a place. One will praise students for acting in accord with ecological responsibilities— collecting cans and bottles for recycling, for example; one refrains from praising them, perhaps even chastises or punishes them, for acting out of accord with these responsibilities—discarding candy wrappers on the playground, for example.

Second, one provides them with models—*including oneself*—who do act in accord with their ecological responsibilities. Since visual representation is virtually as effective as live models, one might show the students films of persons and companies acting in an ecologically responsible manner.

Third, one seeks the internalization of these tendencies. One tries to induce in students the tendency to act on them even when the external reinforcers are no longer present—or at least, when they believe they are no longer present. The best strategy for accomplishing this is for a person who treats the children with respect and affection to combine discipline and modeling with an enunciation of ecological standards which they can perceive as applying to instances in question.

Already, then, we are at the point of cultivating in the student a cognitive structure for ecological responsibility. The teaching of such a structure requires, in the first place, that one teach the child the *concepts* to be used in the enunciation of standards of ecological responsibility—the concept of stewardship, for example. It requires, second, that one teach the child how to apply these concepts, by enunciating standards for him or her which make use of the concepts and by evaluating various specimens of ecological responsibility or irresponsibility. And it requires, in the third place, that one give the child *reasons* for these standards. One shows how these standards are related to what God asks of us, his human creatures.

But of course our concern is that this cognitive structure for ecological responsibility be *internalized*, not just be treated as an intellectual game. How can this be done? How can we cultivate the internalization of a cognitive structure for ecological responsibility? How can we cultivate in the student the tendency to *act on* the standards belonging to such a structure? We know the answer. We combine enunciation of the standards with appropriate discipline for their violation. (Increasingly our legal structure is beginning to do this.) And we provide the student with models who enunciate these standards, who try to act on them, and who express their regret when they fail to live up to them and their satisfaction when they do.

Finally, once the beginnings of an internalized cognitive structure for ecological responsibility are found within the student, one practices with him or her the counterpart of moral casuistry, showing in detail the application of the general principles to various specific types of situations.

The psychological evidence discussed in Part Two leads to the conclusion that a program of this sort will be effective in helping to cultivate ecologically responsible action in students, though it will not *guarantee* it. Of course, it presupposes that teachers accept their own ecological responsibility in the form of themselves having, and acting on, a correct cognitive structure for ecological responsibility. Often *there is* the rub!

PART THREE:

A Popular Alternative

11

The Strategy of Values Clarification

As a contrast to the conclusions of Part Two, we shall now look at one currently popular strategy for tendency learning—the so-called *values clarification* strategy. We shall consider this as described by its originators, Louis E. Raths, Merill Harmin, and Sidney B. Simon, in their book *Values and Teaching* (Merrill, 1966; all the page numbers in what follows refer to this book). As they describe values clarification, it obviously fits within the maturational ideology.

From the outset it is clear that Raths *et al.* have what might be called a "mental health" orientation. Their goal is to assist in the production of positive, enthusiastic, purposeful, proud (PEPP) individuals (p. 5). At the end of the introduction, after summarizing their strategy, the authors say that

> many students have been helped to become more purposeful, more enthusiastic, more positive, and more aware of what is worth striving for. This, of course, is the kind of behavior teachers and parents have wanted to promote for some time but, until recently, clear procedures based on adequate theory have not been available (p. 12).

Raths *et al.* hold an inhibitionist version of maturational theory. Internal factors, they believe, prevent many persons from having the desired traits. And *one* very important inhibiting factor is lack of clarity in values. Human beings are to be visualized as ordered on a continuum, with "PEPP" individuals on one end, and those who distinctly lack these traits on the other. "If we define 'values' as those elements that show how a person has decided to use his life, it would be as if the first group's members knew what they valued and the members of the second group had very unclear values" (p. 6). So it is to overcome the blockage caused by unclarity in values that they propose strategies for values clarification, thus to assist in the production of individuals who have the desirable "PEPP" traits.

But what do Raths *et al.* have in mind when they speak of "values?" We quoted one definition above, but let us look more closely at the concept:

> Persons have experiences; they grow and learn. Out of experiences may come certain general guides to behavior. These guides tend to give direction to life and may be called values. Our values show what we tend to do with our limited time and energy. Since we see values as growing from a person's experiences, we would expect that different experiences would give rise to different values and that any one person's values would be modified as his experiences accumulate and change.... As guides to behavior, values evolve and mature as experiences evolve and mature.... After a sufficient amount of hammering, certain patterns of evaluating and behaving tend to develop (pp. 27f.).

In other words, a given person's values are the goals that person has in fact adopted for action, not the goals that *ought to* be adopted. It might be clearer, then, to speak of goals rather than of values, and of goals clarification rather than *values* clarification.

They go on: "In this book we shall be less concerned with the particular value outcomes of any one person's experiences than we will with the process that he uses to obtain his values" (p. 28). They see values as based on three processes. *Choosing:* (1) freely, (2) from alternatives, (3) after thoughtful consideration of the consequences of each alternative. *Prizing:* (4) cherishing, being happy with the choice, and (5) willing to affirm the choice publicly. *Acting:* (6) doing something with the choice, (7) repeatedly, in some pattern of life. "Those processes," they say, "collectively define valuing. Results of the valuing process are called values" (p. 30).

To practice the values-clarification strategy, then, is to do the following:

1. Encourage children to make choices, and to make them freely.
2. Help them discover and examine available alternatives when faced with choices.

3. Help children weigh alternatives thoughtfully, reflecting on the consequences of each.
4. Encourage children to consider what it is that they prize and cherish.
5. Give them opportunities to make public affirmations of their choices.
6. Encourage them to act, behave, live in accordance with their choices.
7. Help them to examine repeated behaviors or patterns in their life (p. 39).

Surely a great deal more is involved in the successful use of this strategy than *clarification*. In fact, it involves the inculcation of tendencies in students—albeit, ones which they themselves have presumably chosen. The term "clarification" is no less misleading than the term "values."

Raths *et al.* add that "the intent of this process is to help children... clarify for themselves what they value. This is very different from trying to persuade children to accept some predetermined set of values" (p. 39). And they ask, rhetorically,

> Why must teachers see their role only as putting things into the mind of the child? Why can't a role be defined that would help a child take all the confusion that already exists in his mind, remove it, look at it, examine it, turn it around, and make some order out of it? Why can't teachers learn to spend some of their time helping children understand what the bewildering array of beliefs and attitudes that saturate our modern life are all about and which suits him best? Is this not the road to values, to *clear* and *personal* values? (p. 45).

This passage tacitly contrasts their strategy of values clarification with strategies whereby the teacher seeks to inculcate values that he or she regards as desirable. The suggestion is in the air that clarification is both more moral than inculcation and more effective in achieving the desirable "PEPP" traits. This comes out even more clearly in another passage, in which they describe their approach as

> based on a conception of democracy that says persons can learn to make their own decisions. It is also based on a conception of humanity that says human beings hold the possibility of being thoughtful and wise and that the

most appropriate values will come when persons use their intelligence freely and reflectively to define their relationships with each other and with an ever-changing world. Furthermore, it is based on the idea that values are personal things if they exist at all . . . that they cannot be of much significance if they do not penetrate the living of the person who holds them (p. 39).[1]

Readers will notice a heavily moralistic tone to this passage and to much of what Raths *et al.* say on this matter. Values inculcation, unlike values clarification, amounts to selling, pushing, urging, forcing your own pet values upon children. It has the air of indoctrination. Free inquiry, thoughtfulness, reason, seem to be lost. Inculcation cannot lead to values that represent the free and thoughtful choice of intelligent humans. It is the teacher's responsibility to support the child's refusal to choose a goal. And so forth. It is ironic that Raths *et al.* should resort to

---

[1]Note here the ideology of the maturationist. The authors go on to compare their approach with earlier strategies: "With each of the above approaches there is the idea of persuasion. The 'right' values are predetermined and it is one method or another of selling, pushing, urging those values upon others. All the methods have the air of indoctrination, with some merely more subtle than others. The idea of free inquiry, thoughtfulness, reason seems to be lost. The approach seems not to be how to help the child develop a valuing process but, rather, how to persuade the child to adopt the 'right' values" (p. 41). "We have no doubt that such methods as those listed . . . have in the past controlled behavior and even formed beliefs and attitudes, but we assert that they have not *and cannot* lead to values in the sense that we are concerned with them—values that represent the free and thoughtful choice of intelligent humans interacting with complex and changing environments" (p. 40). "It should be increasingly clear that [in our strategy] the adult does not force his own pet values upon children. What he does is create conditions that aid children in finding values *if* they choose to do so. When operating with this value theory, it is entirely possible that children will choose not to develop values. It is the teacher's responsibility to support this choice also, while at the same time realizing that value development is likely to be one of the goals of the school . . ." (p. 47). "Corruption is not an unusual occurrence. So many people can be 'bought.' Does this not suggest that the approaches to values that have been so widely used in the past have been less than effective? Adults have been trying to set examples for years. They have tried often with ingenious manipulation to persuade children to accept certain values. They have carefully limited choices given to children. They have attempted to inspire identification with particular values. They have made rules and insisted on certain patterns of behavior. They have relied upon religion and cultural truisms. They have appealed to the consciences of young people. But even a casual look at the results of these approaches is discouraging. They just do not seem to have worked" (p. 44).

such oppressively hortatory language to try to inculcate in teachers the value of not seeking in turn to inculcate values in children. It is not merely ironic but contradictory for them to urge teachers not to inculcate their own values in students while at the same time urging teachers to *encourage* children to make choices, to *encourage* children to consider what it is that they prize and cherish, and to *encourage* them to act in accord with their choices. And so we have the spectacle of someone passionately urging teachers to avoid inculcating their values while with equal passion urging them to inculcate in children the value of clarifying their values—all for the sake of the values that Raths *et al.* hold so dear: being "PEPP."

In spite of the overwhelmingly clear suggestion that the teacher would be *wrong* to engage in values inculcation, and *wrong* not to engage in values clarification, the official basis of what Raths *et al.* say is either ethical egoism or antinomianism—most likely the latter. It is worth quoting a decisive passage at length:

> If a child says that he likes something, it does not seem appropriate for an older person to say, "You shouldn't like that." Or, if a child should say, "I am interested in that," it does not seem quite right for an older person to say to him, "You shouldn't be interested in things like that." If these things have grown out of a child's experience, they are consistent with his life. When we ask him to deny his own life, we are in effect asking him to be a hypocrite. We seem to be saying in an indirect way, "Yes, this is what your life has taught you, but you shouldn't say so. You should pretend that you had a different life." What are we doing to children when we put them into positions like this? Are we helping them to develop values or are we in effect saying that life is a fraud and that one should learn to live like a fraud very early in life?
>
> We have an alternative approach to values, ... It is important to note that our definition of values and valuing leads to a conception of these words that is highly personal. It follows that if we are to respect a person's life, we must respect his experience and his right to help in examining it for values.

As a matter of fact, in a society like ours, governed by our Constitution, teachers might well see themselves as obliged to support the idea that every individual is entitled to the views that he has and to the values that he holds, especially where these have been examined and affirmed. Is this not the cornerstone of what we mean by a free society? As teachers, then, we need to be clear that we cannot dictate to children what their values should be since we cannot also dictate what their environments should be and what experiences they will have. We may be authoritative in those areas that deal with truth and falsity. In areas involving aspirations, purposes, attitudes, interests, beliefs, etc., we may raise questions, but we cannot "lay down the law" about what a child's values should be. By definition and by social right, then, values are personal things (pp. 36f.).

There is much about this passage that is bewildering. Apparently everybody *ought* to respect the *rights* of others and nobody should be asked to be a hypocrite. Yet what mainly comes through is that no one should judge another person's values as right or wrong (one wonders whether it would be *wrong* to do so; what is the force of their view that it is "not appropriate"). *Neither should the person judge his or her own values by reference to the categories of right and wrong.* One must simply calculate which will be most satisfying.[2] Apparently the claim is that the concepts of *right* and *wrong* do not even apply to actions.

This antinomian interpretation is confirmed when we look at the samples of values clarification that Raths *et al.* offer. Nowhere in the model does the teacher suggest that the student consider what would be *right* to do—not even, what would be *right for him or her* to do. In this the models are faithful to the formulation of the decisive stage (4) in the strategy. The teacher is not to encourage children to consider what would be right to do, but to "encourage children to consider what it is that they

---

[2]Compare this remark (p. 28): "These ideas grow from the assumption that whatever values one obtains should work as effectively as possible to relate one to his world in a satisfying and intelligent way." Again, what is the force of "should" here?

prize and cherish." The following model offered by Raths *et al.* is a good sample of the strategy in practice (pp. 72f.):

> *Teacher:* You were late again today. Do you like coming to school late?
>
> *Student:* Well, no.
>
> *Teacher:* How long have you been coming to school late?
>
> *Student:* Quite a while. I guess most of the time since I've been coming to school.
>
> *Teacher:* How do you feel about being tardy?
>
> *Student:* Well, I feel funny about it sometimes.
>
> *Teacher:* What do you mean by "funny?"
>
> *Student:* Well, that I'm different from other kids. I feel embarrassed.
>
> *Teacher:* As I get it, you feel uncomfortable about being late.
>
> *Student:* That's right.
>
> *Teacher:* What can I do to help you get here on time?
>
> *Student:* Well, my mother usually calls me in the morning—but sometimes she oversleeps.
>
> *Teacher:* Do you have an alarm clock?
>
> *Student:* No.
>
> *Teacher:* Could you get one? I could help you get one if that is what you think you need.
>
> *Student:* It would be kind of fun. I'll try to get one.

The antinomianism of Raths *et al.* comes out most clearly when they raise the question as to whether children should be allowed to choose anything they wish. Their answer is No. Parents and teachers have the right (*sic*) to set certain choices as off-limits. But Raths *et al.* never suggest that adults have the right because those choices would be wrong. It is rather because those choices would be *intolerable* to parents or teachers. Thus does antinomianism turn into arbitrary authoritarianism. Parents and teachers have the right to forbid certain choices; but not because those choices are wrong, simply because they are not to the taste of parents or teachers (who, it should be noted, have the power to enforce their will). The following model is instructive (pp. 114f.):

> *Teacher:* So some of you think it is best to be honest on tests, is that right? (Some heads nod affirma-

tively.) And some of you think dishonesty is all right? (A few hesitant and slight nods.) And I guess some of you are not certain. (Heads nod.) Well, are there any other choices or is it just a matter of dishonesty vs. honesty?

Sam: You could be honest some of the time and dishonest some of the time.

Teacher: Does that sound like a possible choice, class? (Heads nod.) Any other alternatives to choose from?

Tracy: You could be honest in some situations and not in others. For example, I am not honest when a friend asks about an ugly dress, at least sometimes. (Laughter)

Teacher: Is that a possible choice, class? (Heads nod again.) Any other alternatives?

Sam: It seems to me that you have to be all one way or all the other.

Teacher: Just a minute, Sam. As usual we are first looking for the alternatives that there are in the issue. Later we'll try to look at any choice that you may have selected. Any other alternatives, class? (No response.) Well, then, let's list the four possibilities that we have on the board and I'm going to ask that each of you do two things for yourself: (1) see if you can identify any other choices in this issue of honesty and dishonesty, and (2) consider the consequences of each alternative and see which ones you prefer. Later, we will have buzz groups in which you can discuss this and see if you are able to make a choice and if you want to make your choice part of your actual behavior. That is something you must do for yourself.

Ginger: Does that mean that we can decide for ourselves whether we should be honest on tests here?

Teacher: No, that means that you can decide on the value. I personally value honesty; and although you may choose to be dishonest, I shall insist that we be honest on our tests here. In other areas of your life, you may have more freedom to be dishonest, but one can't do *anything any time,* and in this class I shall expect honesty on tests.

Ginger: But then how can we decide for ourselves? Aren't you telling us what to value?

Sam: Sure, you're telling us what we should do and believe in.

Teacher: Not exactly. I don't mean to tell you what you should value. That's up to you. But I do mean that in this class, not elsewhere necessarily, you have to be honest on tests or suffer certain consequences. I merely mean that I cannot give tests without the rule of honesty. All of you who choose dishonesty as a value may not practice it here, that's all I'm saying. Further questions anyone?

Raths *et al.* began by recommending values clarification as a therapeutic strategy for overcoming internal inhibitions, so that those who do not have the desirable mental health traits of "PEPP" can acquire them. But once they are well into the book it becomes clear that values clarification is being recommended also as a preventive strategy. Values clarification is said to prevent the rise of various inhibitions which block people off from acquiring the desirable "PEPP" traits.

In summary, the values clarification strategy as propounded by its founders is set within the context of a maturational inhibitionist theory of education. The strategy consists of doing things which will induce students to go through the seven steps, with respect to some choice in reality or in imagination. The aim of the strategy, briefly expressed, is to get students to outline alternative actions, to reflect on the consequences of these, and to choose one of them by considering which they expect to find most satisfying. The teacher is apparently free to apply the strategy to any potential choice of the students; in fact, of course, it will be those potential choices the teacher considers important or interesting which will be selected. The "good" that the teacher aims at in applying the strategy is just success in taking students through the seven steps. This outcome may be briefly, though misleadingly, described as clarification of values. According to the theory, clear values contribute to the formation of those desirable traits which together constitute mental health, which in turn is the proper goal of education.

Before plunging in and using the strategy of values clarification for the purpose intended, one must pose two fundamental questions: Is the end for which the strategy is intended—the production of "PEPP" individuals—desirable? And is the strategy effective in achieving that end? Let us concentrate on the second question first. Here a most astonishing thing turns up. Raths *et al.* confess that no one knows whether the strategy is effective. They cite a few experiments which they regard as relevant, but they themselves admit (in their chapter on research evidence) that the evidence is thoroughly incomplete and indecisive. So we are being passionately urged to adopt a strategy for securing a result when those doing the urging admit that there is no good evidence that it will in fact secure the result.

The values clarification strategy consists, in essence, of getting students to become clear on what they would like to do (feel comfortable in doing) in an actual or hypothetical situation, and then in exhorting them to act thus when the situation arises. The truth is that there is no good reason whatever to think that classroom exercises of this sort will tend to produce "PEPP" individuals. It is sheer bluff on the part of Raths *et al.* to suggest, as they often do, that their proposals are backed up by solid evidence.[3] Indeed, I suspect that when practiced on certain types of students, with respect to certain sorts of issues, the use of values clarification strategy produces intense inner conflict and anxiety.

But suppose, on the other hand, that classroom exercises of this sort did tend to produce "PEPP" individuals (note, by the way, how unmistakably "American" is this image of the ideal personality). Then it is worth observing that there is no particular connection between being a personality of this type and being a responsible agent. More successful con-artists are probably positive, enthusiastic, purposeful, and proud than saints are. We have suggested that the proper ultimate goal of education is responsible action on the part of the student. Even if the strategy of values clarification were effective for achieving its stated goal of producing individuals with the "PEPP" traits, it would at best be

---

[3]Here, for example, is what they say already on p. 4: "Could it be that a number of children's problems currently attributed to emotions, for example, are more usefully seen as resulting from value disturbances? The study and research upon which this book is based answers that question affirmatively. We have found that. . . ."

marginally relevant to the proper goal of tendency learning, namely, responsible action. That should come as no surprise, for the strategy explicitly repudiates raising the question of what it would be right to do.

We have seen that the values clarification strategy, as formulated by its founders, is antinomian. It is internally incoherent. It is without any basis in evidence. It is pointed toward a very different educational goal from that of Christian education, and of responsibility theory in general. Yet there will be those who want to know whether there is some way the insights of Raths *et al.* can be put to use in the context of Christian education. Suppose, for example, that it were modified to the extent of making the question posed in the decisive fourth step not "What would you feel comfortable in doing?" but "What do you think would be right to do?" Would it then have some use?

Possibly so. But only, I think, a subordinate use. For the responsible educator goes beyond asking the students what they think would be right to do and then urging them to do it. Such a procedure would be, in effect, to urge each person to do what is right in his or her own eyes, and that is scarcely better than urging each person to do what he or she would feel comfortable doing. That might sound merely silly if applied to educational theory; it would be downright dangerous if our legislators were to accept it as a recommendation for law-making—as the chaotic experience of ancient Israel during the period of the biblical judges amply attests.

Reflections on Taxonomy

Reflections on Taxonomy

A great deal of discussion among educationists in recent years has focused on what is referred to as the *taxonomy of educational goals*. Much of this was stimulated by the detailed taxonomy developed by Benjamin S. Bloom, of the University of Chicago, and his associates, their first publication appearing in 1956. A taxonomy of educational goals is simply a classification of those goals based on what one judges to be structurally significant similarities and differences among them.[1] Since our discussion of education for responsible action has made certain assumptions about taxonomy, it may be worthwhile to discuss a few of the issues involved in taxonomies of educational goals, and then compare Bloom's taxonomy with our own.

Teachers often aim at having students actually do certain things in the classroom. One might call these *performance goals*. Some of these performances are desired because the teacher wishes to bring about or test for other goals which are not performances, namely, enduring alterations in the students. Other performance goals are desired not so much for educational reasons as to make the classroom a humane, decent, pleasant place to be in. Such goals, though certainly important, are not uniquely educational. Thus more fundamental than performance goals to what is unique in the educational process are *alteration* goals. At the heart

---

[1]A distinction is made between "classification" and "taxonomy." As Bloom notes: "While a classification scheme may have many arbitrary elements, a taxonomy scheme may not. A taxonomy must be so constructed that the order of the terms must correspond to some 'real' order among the phenomena represented by the terms"; Bloom *et al.*, *Taxonomy of Educational Objectives*, I (Longman, 1956), 17. A classification may be more or less taxonomic. Some of its classifications may be of structural significance and others may not be. Thus a classification scheme may be taxonomic at some points while at others it is not.

of what is unique to education is the fact that teachers aim to produce enduring alterations in their students.

We began by suggesting that most of the alterations at which teachers characteristically aim can be classified under a tripartite distinction of knowledge, ability, and tendency. Teachers aim at increasing the child's knowledge on certain matters, developing certain abilities in the child, and cultivating certain tendencies in the child. I tacitly assumed that this distinction is psychologically tenable. I argued that a responsibility theory of education—and in particular, a *Christian* theory of education— would regard it as important for the teacher to have goals under each of these headings, though I did not contend that *all* enduring alterations at which teachers do aim—nor even at which a *Christian* teacher should aim—can be fitted under these three. I argued only that these are characteristic of teachers, and that goals of these sorts will have a prominent place in a program of education which has a Christian orientation. The remainder of the discussion then concentrated on goals concerning tendencies.

So I have presupposed a taxonomy of educational goals. Or rather, I have presupposed the topmost distinction in a taxonomy of educational goals, not an entire detailed taxonomy. Now the construction of a taxonomy presupposes a *multiplicity* of goals. Otherwise, the issue of a structurally significant classification of them could not arise. Someone, seeing this, might ask why it is not enough for the Christian educator to have as his or her goal to promote responsible action. Why would he or she ever be led into holding a multiplicity of goals? In short, why is a taxonomy even relevant?

Quite simple. For designing curricula, for working out lesson plans, for conducting the sort of discussion which this book represents, for constructing tests, the educator finds it necessary to have the goal of promoting responsible action expressed in more detail. That goal is a unified complex, a complexity within unity, and if educators are to make the choices that face them, they need some of this complexity unraveled. The actual process of education requires specificity of curriculum goals and lesson objectives.

But once a detailed set of goals and objectives has been derived, it is then important to perceive their relationships and note their structural connections, or we will have nothing but disparate shards. And once the structural connections have been noted, a taxonomy can be constructed to display them. One of the major benefits of a taxonomy of the educational goals appropriate to a program of Christian education is that it displays the structural connections of those various detailed goals. Without it the connections of the detailed goals to each other and to the ultimate goal threaten to go unnoticed.

A taxonomy can also serve to call one's attention to worthwhile goals one might otherwise overlook or forget. It can correct misplaced emphases. As Bloom remarks, educators can look on a taxonomy as specifying a range of educational goals which it is possible for them to adopt for themselves, with the result that "comparing the goals of their present curriculum with the range of possible outcomes may suggest additional goals they may wish to include."[2]

Constructing a taxonomy of the proper goals for Christian day school education is of distinctly secondary importance for Christian education, however. A taxonomy presupposes decisions about what those goals are, and those decisions are vastly more important than developing a structure for them. Furthermore, taxonomies pose serious dangers in the hands of imperceptive educators. For one thing, a taxonomy may conceal the many points at which educators themselves must make decisions concerning goals. As Bloom observes,

> there was some concern expressed in the early meetings that the availability of the taxonomy might tend to abort the thinking and planning of teachers with regard to curriculum, particularly if teachers merely selected what they believed to be desirable objectives from the list provided in the taxonomy. The process of thinking about educational objectives, defining them, and relating them to teaching and testing procedures was regarded as a very important step on the part of teachers. It was suggested that the taxonomy could be most useful to teachers who have already gone through some of the steps in thinking about educational objectives and curriculum.[3]

[2] *Ibid.*, p. 2.
[3] *Ibid.*, pp. 5f.

The temptation, once a taxonomy is in hand, is for educators to apply it in mindless and wooden fashion, insisting that each lesson plan have at least one goal that fits under each of the taxonomic categories and assuming that if this condition is met one has a satisfactory set of goals for that educational unit. Scarcely anything could be more misguided. An educator can decide *which* goals to have under a certain category on a certain occasion—and whether to have any goals at all under that category—only by reference to considerations external to the taxonomy and its adoption. Then, too, no existing taxonomy of educational goals makes any pretense of completeness. Accordingly, there may well be goals good and appropriate for a given piece of education which find no place in the taxonomy. Only if one keeps these dangers vividly in mind will it be beneficial to adopt a taxonomy.

Working with a taxonomy gives rise to another danger. Sometimes it is said that the proper goal of education is to educate the whole child—the *entire* child with all the *interrelated* facets of his or her being. It has been suggested that a taxonomy tends to make us overlook that wholeness.[4] For example, once one has taken as fundamental the distinction between the cognitive domain and the affective, the temptation arises that one will think of these as having little or nothing to do with one another. Overall, a taxonomy is based as much on perceiving commonalities as differences, but when one gets to the *ultimate* distinction that the taxonomy makes, it is the differences that are highlighted. Various goals are *grouped together*, say, as cognitive, and some commonality is thereby called to our attention. But no commonality is called to our attention between those grouped under cognitive and those grouped under affective. To counteract this danger, one must constantly keep before educators who use a taxonomy the interrelations of the various sorts of goals found in the taxonomic structure.

An alteration goal, we said, is the goal of producing a certain change in the knowledge, the abilities, the habits, the

---

[4]Cf. Bloom, *ibid.*, pp. 5f.: "Some fear was expressed that the taxonomy might lead to fragmentation and atomization of educational purposes such that the parts and pieces finally placed into the classification might be very different from the more complete objective with which one started."

feelings, etc., of the student. But the change to be produced is a change with respect to a certain range of subject matter—to increase the student's knowledge with respect to economics or to increase the student's skill with respect to piano playing. In short, every educational goal is the goal of producing a psychic change of a certain sort with respect to a certain subject matter. Thus there is room for two very different sorts of taxonomies of educational goals: *pedagogical* taxonomies and *curricular* taxonomies. Pedagogical taxonomies classify the various sorts of *psychic* changes that the goals are concerned with; curricular taxonomies classify the various *subject matter* changes that the goals are concerned with. Since to educate always means to educate *someone* concerning *something*, curricular and pedagogical taxonomies are equally relevant for the educator. My distinction between cognitive, ability, and tendency goals constitutes the topmost classification in a *pedagogical* not a curricular taxonomy. That fits with the fact that this is an essay in pedagogy not curriculum.

Suppose, now, that a taxonomy is proposed. How does one go about evaluating it? How does one decide whether or not the similarities and dissimilarities on which it is based are significant?

Let me speak first of pedagogical taxonomies. A pedagogical taxonomy uses a battery of concepts about the human self. Do those concepts mark out tenable distinctions? If they do, how are the differentiated phenomena related? These questions can be answered only by psychological theory.[5] Bloom's taxonomy, for instance, takes as one of its ultimate distinctions that between inducing changes in cognition and inducing changes in affect. Only psychological theory can tell us whether that distinction between cognition and affect is a tenable one. Maybe even a relatively unsophisticated psychological theory can give us the answer, but the more sophisticated the theory, and the better grounded its claims, the more reliable its answers.

What this means is that pedagogical taxonomies are not

---

[5]"A classification scheme may be validated by reference to the criteria of communicability, usefulness and suggestiveness; while a taxonomy must be validated by demonstrating its consistency with the theoretical views in research finding of the field it attempts to order"; *ibid.*, p. 17.

theory-neutral. They commit themselves, they take a position, on matters which fall within the domain of psychological theory. Of course a pedagogical taxonomy devised by someone who accepts one psychological theory may be identical in all important respects to one devised by someone who accepts another psychological theory. It may be that the psychological theory used in constructing a pedagogical taxonomy is not *as a whole* presupposed by that taxonomy, so that one could accept the taxonomy without accepting the entire psychological theory of the person who formulated it. What we should say about pedagogical taxonomies, then, is not that they *presuppose* one or another specific psychological theory but that they *make commitments* of significance for theoretical psychology, in the sense that there will be psychological theories which find the taxonomy unacceptable in one or another of its features. To put it another way, pedagogical taxonomies are not so much "theory-laden" as "theory-committed."

But a psychological theory by itself cannot yield a pedagogical taxonomy.[6] It yields a set of concepts and some theories about the relations among the entities falling under them. For a pedagogical taxonomy, we also need judgments as to which affinities and disaffinities among those concepts are more significant and which are less significant. Such judgments can only be made by reference to purposes. Relative to certain purposes, one distinction is more significant than another; relative to another purpose, the importance of those distinctions may be reversed.

[6]"In discussing the principles by which a taxonomy might be developed, it was agreed that the taxonomy should be an educational-logical-psychological classification system. The terms in this order express the emphasis placed on the different principles by which the taxonomy could be developed. Thus, first importance should be given to educational considerations. Insofar as possible, the boundaries between categories should be closely related to the distinctions teachers make in planning curricula or in choosing learning situations. It is possible that teachers make distinctions which psychologists would not make in classifying or studying human behavior. However, if one of the major values of the taxonomy is in the improvement of communication among educators, then educational distinctions should be given major consideration. Second, the taxonomy should be a logical classification in that every effort should be made to define terms as precisely as possible and to use them consistently. Finally, the taxonomy should be consistent with relevant and accepted psychological principles and theories"; *ibid.*, p. 6.

Of course, the psychologist has a purpose—to construct theories. By reference to that purpose, the whole scheme of concepts acquires a significance-structure which the psychologist could display in a taxonomy of the concepts appearing in the theory. But the pedagogical taxonomist is dealing with educational purposes, and these differ from those of the psychologist. For the purpose of the educator some psychological distinctions may be more significant, others less so, than for the psychologist. Thus the significance-structure of the psychological concepts used in formulating educational purposes may be different from the significance-structure of those same concepts when used by a theoretical psychologist.

What follows from this is that if one wants to assess a pedagogical taxonomy one must first judge—by reference to one's own psychological theory—whether or not the psychological distinctions it makes are tenable and the relationships it tacitly claims to hold among the entities classified are real. Then one must judge whether the taxonomy does in fact pick out those similarities and dissimilarities which one judges significant for the purposes of the educator. If (to cite a rather old-fashioned example) a pedagogical taxonomy takes as its basic distinction the difference between changes in intellect, changes in emotion, and changes in will, that taxonomy will be acceptable only to someone holding a psychological theory in which that is a tenable distinction and only to someone who believes that for the purposes of an educator it is a distinction of basic significance.

Similarly for curricular taxonomies. One can compose a curricular taxonomy only if one has a theory about the conceptual structure of the subject matter—a theory of scientific structure or of some segment of scientific structure. Correspondingly, a curricular taxonomy will be theory-committed on such matters. It will be acceptable only to someone whose theory of scientific structure accepts the distinctions made and the relations tacitly claimed. Again, the theory of scientific structure does not itself yield a curricular taxonomy. To construct a curricular taxonomy one must make judgments as to which similarities and dissimilarities are more important for the educator, given his or her purposes, to make, and which are less important. The structure of mathematics may look quite different from the standpoint of the educator's purposes from how it looks from the standpoint of the theoretical mathematician's purposes.

Finally, it must not be supposed that theories of psychology, theories of scientific structure, and judgments about important educational distinctions enter the picture for the first time when, the educators having formulated their goals, the taxonomists come along to classify them. Quite to the contrary. In the contemporary world educators formulate their own goals with such theories and judgments in mind. Not only are taxonomies committed on matters of theory and significance-structure. So too are the formulations of the goals which the taxonomist proposes to classify. Goal formulation, theorizing, significance-structuring for the educator's purposes, and taxonomy construction are all intertwined.

*   *   *

The items for which Bloom *et al.* attempted to construct a taxonomy were acquired by going to persons involved in the educational enterprise and collecting statements of their educational goals. This was purported to be a wholly impartial accumulation, and at no point did Bloom *et al.* explicitly make judgments about the acceptability or even the importance of the goals thus accumulated.[7] The classification itself was to be a purely descrip-

---

[7]This is what they say: "It was further agreed that in constructing the taxonomy effort should be made to avoid value judgments about objectives and behaviors. Neutrality with respect to educational principles and philosophies was to be achieved by constructing a system which, insofar as it was possible, would permit the inclusion of objectives from all educational orientations"; *ibid.*, pp. 6f. However, to see how very far indeed they are from achieving this goal, indeed, how impossible it is, consider this passage in which they are speaking about their classification of affective goals: "It is difficult to describe the behaviors appropriate to these objectives since the internal or covert feelings and emotions are as significant for this domain as are the overt behavioral manifestations." Skinnerian behaviorists would regard this statement as flatly false. For them, feelings and emotions are of no theoretical significance whatever; all that counts, in well-formed theory, is observable behavior. Thus Skinnerian behaviorists would protest before the taxonomy even gets started, at the point where Bloom *et al.* just accept what teachers offer as their goals. A Skinnerian would claim that what teachers say is filled with illusion. Cf. also this: "The taxonomy should be consis-

tive scheme, representing every type of educational goal in a neutral fashion. The aim was

> to make the taxonomy neutral by avoiding terms which implicitly convey value judgments and by making the taxonomy as inclusive as possible. This means that the kinds of behavioral changes emphasized by *any* institution, educational unit, or educational philosophy can be represented in the classification. Another way of saying this is that any objective which describes an intended behavior should be classifiable in this system.[8]

All collected goals would find their place in the system and none would be judged inferior.

The main usefulness of their taxonomy, say Bloom *et al.*, is "to facilitate communication" and to improve "the exchange of ideas and materials among test workers, as well as other persons concerned with educational research and curriculum development."[9] Exchange of information in these areas is often disappointing, "because all too frequently what appears to be common ground between schools disappears on closer examination of the descriptive terms being used."[10]

The hope is that the taxonomy constructed will provide a set of terms with more precise meanings than their ordinary language counterparts, usable by various competing schools of education, thus facilitating communication.[11] But surely such a hope is naive and illusory. Bloom's taxonomy is not a theory-neutral scheme of precisely defined words. It is a theory-committed structuring of the field. Those who dispute its theory-commitments will not, or should not, accept the taxonomy.

The Bloom taxonomy is a *pedagogical* one, not a curricu-

---

tent with our present understanding of psychological phenomena. Those distinctions which are psychologically untenable, even though regularly made by teachers, would be avoided. Further, distinctions which seem psychologically important, even though not frequently made in educational objectives, would be favorably considered for inclusion"; *ibid.*, p. 14.

[8] *Ibid.*, p. 14.

[9] *Ibid.*, p. 10.

[10] *Ibid.*, p. 1.

[11] As to the benefit of this, see David R. Krathwohl *et al.*, *Taxonomy of Educational Objectives*, II (MacKay, 1964), 5f.

lar one.[12] The authors realized that in order to construct a detailed pedagogical taxonomy a background psychological theory is needed.

> We need a method of ordering phenomena such that the method of ordering reveals significant relationships among the phenomena. This is the basic problem of a taxonomy—to order phenomena in ways which will reveal some of their essential properties as well as the interrelationships among them. Members of the taxonomy group spent considerable time in attempting to find a psychological theory which would provide a sound basis for ordering the categories of the taxonomy. We reviewed theories of personality and learning but were unable to find a single view which, in our opinion, accounted for the varieties of behaviors represented in the educational objectives we attempted to classify. . . . What is needed is a larger synthetic theory of learning than at present seems to be available.[13]

Despite this critical lack, they plunged ahead, even suggesting that their work would be useful for future theorizing:

> We are of the opinion that our method of ordering educational outcomes will make it possible to define the range of phenomena for which such a theory must account. The taxonomy also uses an order consistent with research findings and it should provide some clues as to the nature of the theory which may be developed.[14]

The fundamental differentiation in the Bloom taxonomy is between what it calls the cognitive domain, the affective domain, and the psychomotor domain. (Bloom *et al.* have published nothing on the psychomotor domain.) These are sometimes described informally as the domains of thinking, feeling,

---

[12]"It should be noted that we are not attempting to classify the instructional methods used by teachers, the ways in which teachers relate themselves to students, or the different kinds of instructional materials they use. We are not attempting to classify the particular subject matter or content. What we are classifying is the *intended behavior* of students—the ways in which individuals are to act, think, or feel as the result of participating in some unit of instruction"; Bloom, *op. cit.*, p. 12.

[13]*Ibid.*, p. 12.

[14]*Ibid.*, pp. 17f.

and acting. Goals falling within the cognitive domain are those which "deal with the recall or recognition of knowledge and the development of intellectual abilities and skills."[15] Those falling within the affective domain are those dealing with "changes in interest, attitudes, and values, and the development of appreciations and adequate adjustment."[16] Let me here focus my attention on the acceptability of what they say concerning the affective domain.

Among student responses which teachers aim to produce, which fall within the affective domain? Some examples given are being aware of aesthetic factors in things, attending when others speak, listening to music with discrimination, obeying playground regulations, acquainting oneself with current political issues, finding pleasure in reading for recreation, desiring to develop the ability to speak effectively, assuming responsibility for drawing reticent members of a group into conversation, being devoted to the ideals of democracy, forming judgments as to the responsibility of society for conserving resources, weighing alternative social policies against the standards of the public welfare, being ready to revise judgments and change behavior in the light of evidence, and developing a consistent philosophy of life.

Now what is it that these responses have in common, making them all belong within one domain? Unfortunately, Bloom *et al.* never make that decisively clear. Notice that this list of "affective goals" includes several which are clearly *performance* goals and several others which clearly are not. *Listening to music with discrimination* is an action; so too is *obeying playground regulations*. But *desiring to develop the ability to speak effectively* and *being devoted to ideals of democracy* are not actions. It would have aided the cause of clarity immeasurably if Bloom *et al.* had drawn a distinction such as the one I have suggested between *performance* goals and *alteration* goals.

At the very beginning, then, we have to *interpret* Bloom. I suggest that what is really in view here is *not* the action of listening to music with discrimination but something like the

[15] *Ibid.*, p. 7.
[16] *Loc. cit.*

habit of listening to music with discrimination, not the *action* of obeying playground regulations but something like the *tendency* to obey playground regulations. Bloom's affective goals should be construed as alteration goals.

With this interpretation, we can return to our question: What do these goals I have listed have in common? Bloom *et al.* call them all *affects;* and what psychologists characteristically mean by an affect is a feeling, an emotion. One might naturally conclude, then, that Bloom's affective domain is a classification of goals pertaining to the feelings of the student. I think, however, that here too we shall have to *interpret* Bloom.

Bloom *et al.* make it clear that the phenomena which they classify as belonging to the affective domain all involve or consist of *feeling positively* toward something. They agree that there are also affects which involve or consist of feeling negatively toward something. But they suggest that educators rarely seek to produce these in students intentionally. So *affects* for Bloom *et al.* are apparently not feelings and emotions in general but desires, goals, likes, inclinations, pro-attitudes—that sort of thing. One is reminded that the English word "affect" comes from the Latin *affectare*, meaning "to aim at."

This interpretation harmonizes with Bloom's view that one can order affects by assessing the degree to which they cause (or would cause, other things being equal) sustained action on the individual's part. For example, that positive attitude which on Bloom's view constitutes an awareness of the aesthetic factors in things does little (so he says) by way of functioning as a cause of action; whereas that positive attitude which constitutes the desire to develop the ability to speak effectively causes a sustained pattern of action. This ordering of the components

> seemed to describe a process by which a given phenomenon or value passed from a level of bare awareness to a position of some power to guide or control the behavior of a person. If it passed through all the stages in which it played an increasingly important role in a person's life, it would come to dominate and control certain aspects of that life as it was absorbed more and more into the internal controlling structure. This process or continuum seemed best described by a term which was heard at

various times in our discussions and which has been used similarly in the literature: "internalization." This word seemed an apt description of the process by which the phenomenon or value successively and pervasively become a part of the individual.[17]

My suggestion, then, as the reader may have surmised, is that what Bloom means by an *affect* is not far from what I have called a *tendency*. It is not, indeed, identical. Affects are presumably always states of consciousness, affirmative *attitudes*. Tendencies, by contrast, though they may be *accompanied* by states of consciousness, are not themselves to be *identified* with such states. And I daresay that some habitual tendencies do not even have states of consciousness as their accompaniments. One wonders where in his taxonomy Bloom would place habits.

Furthermore, Bloom holds that some affects—for example, awareness of aesthetic factors in things—do not involve tendencies to action. Rather, the degree to which an affect manifests itself in a sustained tendency is, for him, a principle of classification; and some affects manifest no such tendency at all. Then, too, the tendency to act on a principle, which occupies so central a position in the theory we have outlined, finds no place in Bloom's classification. For this tendency of course cannot be understood as simply an affirmative attitude. Incidentally, one wonders why the *awareness* of aesthetic factors in things is thought to constitute an affirmative *attitude?* Is awareness in general an affirmative attitude? How about awareness of pain?

[17]Krathwohl *et al.*, pp. 27f. Cf. p. 33: "The process of internalization can be described by summarizing the continuum at successive levels as they appear in the *Affective Domain Taxonomy*. The process begins when the attention of the student is captured by some phenomenon, characteristic, or value. As he pays attention to the phenomenon, characteristic, or value, he differentiates it from the others present in the perceptual field. With differentiation comes a seeking out of the phenomenon as he gradually attaches emotional significance to it and comes to value it. As the process unfolds he relates this phenomenon to other phenomena to which he responds that also have value. This responding is sufficiently frequent so that he comes to react regularly, almost automatically, to it and to other things like it. Finally the values are interrelated in a structure or view of the world, which he brings as a "set" to new problems. Even from this abstract description it can be seen that the internalization process represents a continuous modification of behavior from the individual's being aware of a phenomenon to a pervasive outlook on life that influences all his actions."

It is perhaps true, nevertheless, that Bloom with his affective domain was attempting to get at what I have called tendencies. Accordingly, if one is willing to submit Bloom's hazy discussion to such heavy interpretations as I have proposed and to sift through the assortment of things which he calls affects, his taxonomy may be of some positive use for the Christian educator and for the responsibility theorist in general. But I would contend that the knowledge/ability/tendency classification is clearer in conception, more comprehensive in scope, more tenable psychologically, and more relevant to the goals of Christian education than Bloom's knowledge/affect/action distinction.

Let me stress in conclusion what I have said again and again in this essay. A program of Christian education will not first of all aim at those states of consciousness which are affirmative attitudes. It will not first of all aim at affects. It will aim instead at responsible *action* with respect to nature, oneself, one's fellow human beings, and God.

Index

DATE DUE

M